GW00854570

LOST IN TRANSLATION

A handbook for information systems in the 21st century

nigel green & carl bate

Evolved
Technologist
Press
New York, NY

Lost in Translation: A handbook for information systems in the 21st century

Nigel Green & Carl Bate

Published by Evolved Technologist Press, an imprint of Evolved Media, 242 West 30th Street, Suite 801, New York, New York 10001

This book may be purchased for educational, business, or sales promotional use. For more information contact:

Evolved Technologist Press
(646) 827-2196
info@EvolvedTechnologist.com
www.EvolvedTechnologist.com

Editor: Dan Woods,
Writers: Dan Safarik, Dan Woods
Production Editor: Deb Gabriel
Cover and Interior Design: Kristin Waring Capgemini and 1106 Design
Illustrator: Rob Romano
First Edition: November 2007

ISBN: 978-0-9789218-4-2; 0-9789218-4-4

Dedications

Nigel Green:
"To the Lost Business Analysts and my long suffering family – Den, Lizzie, and Rosie."

Carl Bate:
"To the spirit of 'TCG-ers' past, present, and future – without whom this book would not exist. And with thanks to Lesley, Jackson, and Anna for joy and inspiration."

Acknowledgements

The authors would like to acknowledge the following for their contributions to the book:

Gareth Bunn

Julian Burnett

Bill Cook

Stuart Curley

David Hunt

Sam Lowe

Andy Mulholland

John Schlesinger

Chris Yapp

Special thanks goes to Adrian Apthorp for his significant contributions to discussions over the fifteen-year gestation of VPEC-T.

In addition the authors would like to acknowledge the contribution of and the inspiration from the many compatriots without whom this book and this work could never exist.

A special thanks to Una Du Noyer for unknowingly coming up with the book title.

Contents

Foreword

We live in an age where technology increasingly pervades all aspects of life. Technology that was barely imaginable a generation ago is now commonplace. It has had a profound impact on how we organize services in public, private, and voluntary sectors. But all is not well.

Many organizations struggle to justify investment in IT. The reputation of the supply side for delivering late and over budget damages credibility. Reaping the benefits of investment is harder than it first seems.

It can often feel like a dialogue of the deaf between the IT professionals and the business leaders. One group talks about SOA, IPv6, SaaS, and SQL for instance, while the other side talks about innovation, transformation, efficiency, and customer service.

The authors of this book bring together many years of experience, reflecting on learning from projects in many sectors. It is their belief that it is in the initiation of dialogue, the communication between the parties, to which ultimately an IT system will be part of the solution, that many of the problems arise.

To illustrate some of the challenges faced, consider a few cameos of problems for which technology solution is sought.

Improving Health

You are asked to build an IT system with two key objectives. First is to support and enhance clinical effectiveness. Second is to improve patient outcomes. The system must support data protection, patient confidentiality, and medical ethics.

Explain what the information system is that supports the following patient example.

A woman aged 38 presents herself for fertility treatment. She has been married twice before. Both marriages broke down after failure to produce a child. Last year she met Mr. Right, who wants a child as much as she does. It hasn't happened.

Her younger sister died from breast cancer last year. There has been no family history of breast cancer.

She has a BMI of 32. She has black coffee, orange juice, and a banana for breakfast. She has a light lunch and cooks in the evening for herself and her man. They both like fish and don't eat red meat. She doesn't smoke. She doesn't snack between meals. She is a light drinker, 15 units per week.

He has a child by a previous relationship but doesn't see the child, who moved abroad with the mother when the child was very young.

Business Continuity

The increase in tensions following a terrorist attack requires the local authority, police, and regional transport to improve communications with a variety of agencies. The experience has shown that many businesses were unprepared for the event and there has been a significant loss of business. Some jobs have been lost in the area and this is spilling out into tensions with the ethnic minorities.

A capital grant has been allocated to build an IT system to improve communications between all the parties. If successful this system will be rolled out to other towns and cities at risk of terrorist events.

Will the system, when operational and debugged, roll out effectively to a similar sized town with a similar ethnic mix?

Mergers and Acquisitions

A branch-based financial services company acquires a direct sales organization in a complementary field. There is little need to shed jobs. However, the CEO wants to integrate existing infrastructures and build an IT system to maximize any synergies and to create a one company culture. Where do you start?

Advertising

A successful print media, radio, and television advertising consultancy branched out some time ago into Web advertising. The staff was poached constantly and the business hasn't developed in the way they hoped. A tipping point has been reached in their core business. They believe that they have 2 years to build credibility and a business in online advertising or they will face serious decline. What would you advise?

Values Espoused and in Practice

Company X is a holding company. The chairman and founder buys and sells organizations within the overall corporate structure in diverse market sectors. There is a very small center. All functions are devolved into the operating businesses.

The Chairman thinks that next year there will be an economic slowdown, and hires a major consultancy to advise him on reducing his cost base to improve resilience if his fears are realized. He is very close to the consultancy in question.

They point out that for an organization of their size they spend twice the level on IT as two organizations that he sees as a benchmark.

You are invited to respond to this finding. How do you go about it?

These examples show many of the types of challenges faced in initiating a dialogue between business and IT. Among these challenges is the open ended or vague description of the problem. The solutions require organizational and individual behavior change. Some have complex stakeholder engagements. There are legal, moral, and ethical issues to be dealt with. Building a business case and measuring benefits is tricky. Technology may be a driver rather than a response.

The danger is that " IT is the answer, now what's the problem." The focus is often on the T, the technology, and less so on the I, the information.

This book redresses that balance. The thinking framework outlined here is aimed not on the IT system, but on the Information System. It does not seek to replace or nullify the engineering disciplines needed to design and deliver the final solution, but aims to address the need for a common language between business and technology people so that what is achieved is "I have a problem, how can IT help?" That is a bold aim. By building a common language and a shared understanding of the information system between the different stakeholders, the authors argue that many of the frustrations felt around IT can be overcome, to the benefit of the economy and the wider society.

Dr. Chris Yapp

Introduction

This book addresses a crisis of communication so entrenched and intractable that many people cease to notice it any more. When business and Information Technology people sit down at a table to solve problems and build new solutions, the outcome is rarely pretty and often the process can be downright unpleasant.

Often, *what* a solution should do for the business is described in the broadest strokes. *How* that solution might be implemented is described in microscopic detail. This book explains how to bridge that gap, so that comprehensive communication leads to better solutions.

It turns out that communicating about technology is much harder than anyone ever realized. The development and use of a wide range of technologies that we collectively describe as Information Technology or "IT" has, over some forty years, changed unimaginably, not just its technical capabilities, but in its role and relationships to business and people as well.

In reality, the use of the term "IT" to describe the technology used by people in business today is out of date. When asked, most people would name the improvements in communication, together with the introduction of the Web, as the most significant changes in recent years, and neither was recognized or included in the origination of the term "IT" in the late '80s and early '90s. The term ICT, standing for Information and Communications Technology, is perhaps more representative, but even that fails to adequately convey the way people relate to and use the various forms of technology now available at work or at home.

If we have trouble with defining the scope and terminology of the topic at this fundamental level, the issues business and IT departments face when working together to provide solutions that the business really wants are even more overwhelming. At the fundamental level, the need to understand the critical business needs, and indeed, what IT can practically deliver, is paramount—but do we have the capability to achieve this? It is the rare company that can claim consistent success in crafting IT to meet business needs. We think communication is at the heart of this inconsistency.

Currently, technology product vendors are rising to the challenge of providing new capabilities, but there has yet to be a corresponding elevation of the *thinking process* of how to design, implement and manage these products to deliver business outcomes in the connected world.

In one respect, the increasing interest and focus on "architecture" is a reflection of this need to approach solutions in a methodical way, starting with the business requirement. But from a more behavioral perspective, traditional IS/IT architecture fails to provide the full answer. This is probably due to its engineering roots and the more recent gravitational pull of IT advancements.

Increasingly, businesses—and therefore the *systems* of business—are both "loosely coupled" and provide "any-to-any" re-combinations, often with some part of the value chain or IT solution external to an enterprise and therefore not under its control. We are lacking the language to describe this world that works both for "the business" and "IT."

People will recognize in VPEC-T elements that apply to both the business requirements-definition process and the application of technology; but its real value lies in how business and technology aspects are brought together to make a cohesive, simplified and yet comprehensive approach to the entire problem.

Andy Mulholland,
Global CTO, Capgemini.

Chapter 1

VPEC-T: A Five-Word Path to Improved Communication

Just imagine for a second that communication between business and Information Technology (IT) was perfect. What would that mean? Business could explain the requirements for a solution and IT would provide it. The requirements would more accurately reflect the needs of the business and the resulting solution would be closer to what was desired. The solution delivered could never be perfect, of course, but if it were just good enough, most businesses would be wildly happy. Then based on experience, the solution could be improved as needed.

This book is about one way to get closer to this simple vision. The thinking framework at the center of this book, VPEC-T, enables the business side of a company to capture requirements for an IT solution more accurately and communicate them more effectively to the IT staff.

By using the idea of the information system and the five words: Values, Policies, Events, Content, and Trust, people can find new ways to come together and resolve the underlying tensions within the information systems in which they participate. The power of VPEC-T has

> *An ancient Chinese proverb says:*
>
> **"We start the journey to wisdom when we call things by the right name."**
>
> *Centuries later, Leonardo da Vinci asserted:*
>
> **"Simplicity is the ultimate sophistication."**
>
> *And more recently, Dee Hock, the founder of Visa International, famously said:*
>
> **"Simple, clear purpose and principles give rise to complex, intelligent behavior. Complex rules and regulations give rise to simple, stupid behavior."**
>
> *It seems we've been wrestling with problems associated with the language we use and how to communicate concepts important to us, ever since we decided to share information. We seem attracted to the apparent eloquence of prose and academic discourse. This often clutters our thinking and buries the very idea we wish to communicate under confusing terminology and ill-defined language—as perhaps Leonardo da Vinci implied. Dee Hock understands the importance of clear and simple language and the effects on desired business outcomes when we are overburdened with unnecessary complexity.*

been proven through real projects and has delivered tangible value. The authors wrote this book so that even more people can benefit from this simple but powerful approach.

Barriers to Communications across Business and IT

Since the middle of the last century, the IT industry has created a whole new language to describe concepts that simply didn't exist before, such as software, databases, the Internet, the Web and so on. This language is now part of our everyday life, and *if used correctly*, helps us describe various useful technologies and technical concepts.

VPEC-T Cheerleading

Throughout this book you will see boxes like this one marked with the VPEC-T megaphone. We call these "Cheerleading Boxes" because they contain the unrestrained enthusiasm that Dan Woods, the American playing the role of editor and consulting writer to this book, has for the idea. These boxes are a compromise that resolves a conflict in Values that arose early in the writing and editing process. Nigel Green and Carl Bate, the British inventors of VPEC-T and the primary authors of the book, tended to couch their language in reserved terms. This reserve was true to the values of Capgemini, but Dan felt that it was at war with effective communication about the value and workings of VPEC-T. Nigel and Carl's Values were oriented toward measured claims. Dan sought to oversimplify and then exaggerate. The compromise reached is that Dan gets to gush wildly about his enthusiasm for VPEC-T inside these boxes, and that Nigel and Carl can keep their content safely apart from such giddiness. So, sis, boom, bah—here it goes.

The people who work in IT never intend to provide solutions that are ill suited to the business. At the beginning of each project, they want to do their best to help their companies succeed. The people on the business side of the equation also start with the best of intentions.

It doesn't seem to matter what business outcome is sought (e.g., reduce cost or increase value), what type of business process design is adopted (e.g., standardized or specialized), or what type of IT solution is adopted—(e.g., a business software package, a custom build or use of "Software as a Service"). The resulting collective effort of business and IT in the "IT enabled business change" program invariably seems to miss the mark.

VPEC-T is the solution to this problem because it gives the business a way to express its desired outcomes and a way for IT to express the art of the possible—on paper—and have a conversation about it. VPEC-T uses the idea of an information system as a model of a "business-IT solution." The information system perspective is one that is concerned with the attitudes and behavior of the business and people involved (Values, Trust), the specific rules that are in place (Policies), and the way the information is represented and flows from one step to another (Content, Events).

What VPEC-T captures is the personality of a solution. The first step is to do therapy on the personality captured. Are any Values or Policies in conflict? Once these are resolved, the business and IT can work together and use this personality to guide the business transformation without going back to the business side to ask questions about every little detail.

VPEC-T also changes your thinking about most complex issues. Once you know VPEC-T and have used it, you are on the search for conflicts in Values or sources that corrode Trust. You wonder if any policies are contradictory. You understand systems by first looking for the real-world Events and business Content that matters. Read on, you won't be disappointed.

The problem, however, is that this IT-based language has crept into the way businesses describe and shape their requirements of an Information System, which steers the discussion between business stakeholders and IT specialists toward the *IT-how* rather than the *Business-Outcome-What*. Furthermore, because of the high degree of specialist knowledge required to understand the myriad technologies available today, business folk often find themselves lost in IT concepts. From a business point of view, the IT guys can over-complicate things. This needless complexity seems more pointless than ever in contrast to our personal lives, in which we use simple and direct IT solutions from Web sites, cell phones, and ever-converging forms of consumer electronics. From the IT specialist's point of view, they can find the requirements discussion hampered by this perspective; they are often left with the feeling that "A little knowledge is dangerous."

This is just one example of many frustrating discussions (for both parties) that take place across the Business-IT boundary. We believe the primary cause is rooted in the "lost in translation" problem between the two worlds.

What if there was a technique to enable business and IT specialists to share a common language? What if the insights gained could be communicated at an appropriate level of detail with the Board? Can the "Business/IT divide" be eliminated?

The premise of this book:

This Business/IT divide is the *raison d'être* of this book. The "business" and the "IT" that it uses all form part of the same system *(Information System)*, made up of people, process, information and technology. Yet, often the "business" and the "IT that it uses" are not seen as an integrated whole. Worse still, it sometimes seems that the business and IT communities work against each other, even as they are charged with collaboration.

The business/IT divide has emerged out of the rapid advancements in IT and the associated need for new language within the IT industry. This rapid evolution in the IT industry has made a beeline for industrialized techniques, such as business-process modeling and IT engineering. This industrialization has done a reasonable job of defining *how* IT should work but has failed to define *what* is really needed—and *why* it's useful. A common understanding of the *what* and *why* aspects of the Information System within a business is critical. Its absence is the key reason that such an apparent business/IT divide exists today.

We lack a simple technique for understanding and communicating all the aspects of an Information System. In the business world, many easy-to-use analysis techniques exist and are accessible to all—and they are often in common usage. Take for example, SWOT (Strengths, Weaknesses, Opportunities, and Threats) analysis. In this framework you analyze every issue by listing the ideas and concerns in each category, and then use the resulting analysis to guide future action and decision-making. Such a process is extremely simple and yet powerful for driving consensus on the shape of a business initiative. But we are missing something analogous in business/IT collaboration. The primary aim of such a technique is simple:

- For the business—to be able to express desired business outcomes in language IT managers can use.
- For IT—to be able to express solutions in language business leaders can use.

The Awful Truth

There are two common patterns for the way that business and IT staff fail to communicate: the Merry-Go-Round and the Blank Stare.

A Merry-Go-Round meeting about gathering requirements for a new business solution starts with someone bringing up a goal for a new system. Then someone objects to it or adds another goal or requirement. Then perhaps an IT person explains what they would do to meet that goal, or how the requirement is impossible to satisfy—or perhaps that IT can do different things the business hasn't even thought of yet. The conversation wanders. A list of requirements starts to appear on a white board. Some of the goals and requirements are broad ("increase sales"); others are detailed ("integrate with Blackberries"). In the best case, a list of goals and requirements is delivered to IT, but what comes back is a solution that is in the shape of what the vendor already offers. The fit is awkward.

In the worst case, usually in an environment of hostility and mistrust, the meeting descends into acrimony. Sarcastic comments lead to nasty objections and recriminations about past failures. The meeting skitters about until someone out of frustration screams, "What are we talking about?" or, "Why are we even talking about this—shouldn't we just use x or y? (where x = a business application package and y = a service delivered over the Web as a 'Software as a Service')."

The other pattern, the Blank Stare, is far more subdued but just as unproductive. In this sort of meeting the business people know they want to improve the support for their business process, and suspect technology can help, but they do not know exactly how to express themselves. The meeting starts with the delivery of high-level requirements, but the business people lose steam. They do not know how to explain what they want because they do not know what's possible. The IT department starts explaining what is possible, but the business people do not understand, and are not always quick to say that. The business people sit there with blank stares that seem to say: "We do not know what you are saying and we do not have anything more to say." In this case, a list of goals and requirements is delivered to IT, but what comes back, again, is a solution that is in the shape of what a vendor already offers or what the IT department has already built. The fit is awkward. The system does not help as much as it could.

And it's little wonder that while such meetings are going on, often other folks in the business are using whatever IT they can—office applications, Web applications, whatever they can get their hands on—just to get the job done.

VPEC-T: The Five Elements of Successful Information Systems Analysis

When used properly, the information-systems perspective as shown in Figure 1-1 provides a common ground for business and IT to discuss what's needed—and what's not needed—and how what's needed will be adopted.

There are 5 critical dimensions to the Information System view—expressed in VPEC-T.

VPEC-T is a simplified and accessible technique that can be adopted by the business stakeholders and users, and IT, to create a shared "thinking" language to guide the joint business-IT decision-making. VPEC-T, just like SWOT, creates a simple process for approaching any problem and describes the resulting analysis.

Fred Brooks on Conceptual Integrity

From: *The Mythical Man-Month: Essays on Software Engineering* by Fred Brooks

> "To make a user-friendly system, the system must have conceptual integrity, which can only be achieved by separating architecture from implementation. A single chief architect (or a small number of architects), acting on the user's behalf, decides what goes in the system and what stays out. A 'super cool' idea by someone may not be included if it does not fit seamlessly with the overall system design. In fact, to ensure a user-friendly system, a system may deliberately provide **fewer** features than it is capable of. The point is that if a system is too complicated to use, then many of its **features** will go unused because no one has the time to learn how to use them."

While SWOT categorizes thinking about an issue in general, exploring the extremes of two dimensions (Strengths vs. Weaknesses, Opportunities vs. Threats), VPEC-T breaks down all the aspects of an Information System into five core dimensions, as shown in Table 1-1.

VPEC-T provides the business and IT specialists a better way to communicate, simplifying the language used to describe the outcome-affecting aspects of the business's entire Information System.

At the highest level, the VPEC-T Thinking Framework is an analysis tool and communication vehicle for business and IT stakeholders to aid decision-making processes. This is in contrast to engineering tools, which are used to implement a decision once it has been taken.

- The VPEC-T Thinking Framework is focused on the analysis of the behavior of people and organizations and their interaction with information systems.

- Its objective is to surface issues and concerns early, and in so doing, avoid costly mistakes.
- It focuses on real-world Events, Content, and Policies, and on the Values of people and organizations, and their Trust relationships.
- It is designed to free analysis activities from engineering rigor, thereby helping decision-makers.
- It is an aid to defining an information-systems strategy.
- It is designed to build in adoption approaches from the outset, thereby materially increasing implementation success.

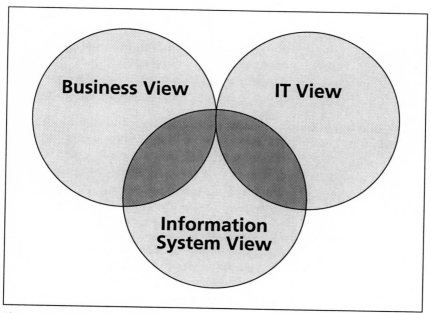

Figure 1-1: Business and IT Connect Via the IS View

At subsequent levels of detail, VPEC-T thinking can be applied to inform detailed design and to guide business transformation endeavors—or it can be applied simply as a things-to-consider-memory-jogger in project reviews.

Dimension	Applying emphasis and techniques to:
Values	Focus on understanding the Values and desired outcomes of both the individual and the business, and the values of individuals and businesses you interact with. Values can be thought of as constraining beliefs (e.g., ethics) and goals (e.g., desired outcomes).
Policies	Focus on the broad range of mandates and agreements such as internal policies, law, external contracts across the business: the rules that govern and constrain how things get done.
Events	Focus on the real-world proceedings that stimulate business activity—sometimes in a pre-defined sequence but often not. These are the triggers for action.
Content	Focus on the documents, conversations, or messages that are produced and consumed by business activities. These are the dialogues we use to share a plan, a concept, a history, and/or the details of a person, place, or thing.
Trust	Focus on fostering Trust between all parties engaged in a system of Value. Trust changes over time, and understanding and fostering Trust relationships are critical to useful IT. The deeper the Trust relationship, the more Values will be authentically disclosed and declared. Trust can be defined as Trust = Intimacy + Credibility / Risk.

Table 1-1: The VPEC-T Dimensions

Why the horrible acronym?

We thought long and hard about what to call our thinking framework for Information Systems. After much discussion and many rejected suggestions, we reverted to a meaningless word that is nevertheless a meaningful acronym—VPEC-T. We found that trying to use the English language's words to describe it just got in the way and overburdened it with inherited meaning. We also found other acronyms to be hollow-sounding, pompous, or full of marketing hype.

So rather than use such words, we invented an abbreviation that reminds us of the five dimensions, but also gives a hint at the relationship between them. We start with the "V" for Values, as that seems to be the foundation for any discussion, in our experience. This is quickly followed by P, for Policies—Values and Policies are close bedfellows. Likewise, Events and Content are really inseparable twins who are great pals of Policies. Then, last, but by no means least, we have Trust, and just before Trust we have a pause—the hyphen (-). Why the pause? We've found that, in order to really uncover the Trust issues and concerns, we need to first have a discussion about the other four dimensions, take stock, and then get to the heart of the Trust issues.

So, it might seem strange that in a book that suggests simplicity of language, we have introduced yet another acronym (the irony is not lost on the authors!), however, we believe VPEC-T is the most authentic and useful name we could have developed. Oh, and one more reason: clients and colleagues are already using the term—it has a life of its own now!

- It is designed to be complementary to proven methods for process and IT requirements/design.
- It helps surface the too-often obscured, outcome-affecting aspects of IT enabled business transformation.

VPEC-T is not a replacement for tried and trusted business-process and IT-engineering methods; rather, it provides an uncomplicated, unifying, business/IT language to complement them. It is specifically designed to support better business/IT collaboration, empowering more relevant and timely executive decision-making about the use of IT.

The "First-First" Mentality

The behavior of the individuals, groups, and automated and non-automated sub-systems are the *real* Information System. This system is usually as dependent on one-on-one conversations and sticky-notes as it is on corporate IT solutions.

Just as the SWOT framework attempts to surround an issue and identify the best and worst cases, VPEC-T surrounds the complex behaviors in an information system and attempts to surface the forces driving that behavior and the flow of information and activity, as shown in Figure 1-2. To improve or otherwise change an information system, all outcome-affecting aspects of the behavior (current and desired) of the Information System must be considered. And it's best to think about them *before* a lot of money is spent on IT.

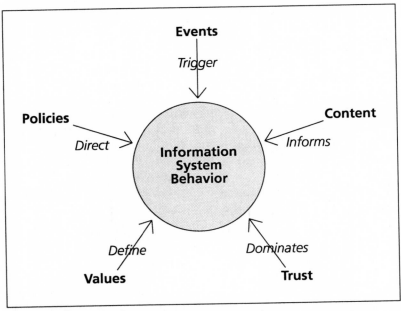

Figure 1-2: Information System Behavior

The Impact of VPEC-T

The focus on behavior produces a wide variety of benefits. Here are some of the results that are commonly achieved by using VPEC-T to structure and focus conversations, analysis, and design:

- Barriers to adoption of IT solutions and opportunities for process improvement are identified and addressed *before* buy or build decisions are made.
- Cultural, organizational, and policy conflicts are surfaced and resolved before the solution is created—instead of just implementing a solution that embeds such conflict in the way the company works.
- The softer, human side of information systems is directly addressed and discussed, which surfaces conflicts and tensions between the Values and Trust relationships.
- The larger landscape in which the information system being created is described, so that the solution can be constructed to meet a wider set of needs.
- The Policies of the information system are made explicit, which provides clear guidance to those implementing the solution, ensuring that business requirements are just that—*requirements*, as opposed to an implementation convenience.
- The Events and Content of the information system are made explicit, which tends to move the architecture of the solution toward an Event-driven approach that makes the solution flexible, and integration with other systems much easier.
- Adoption becomes much less of a struggle, because business users recognize the way they actually work in the solutions created.

Just about any sharing of information between people using any tool is an Information System—imagine applying the five dimensions to an Information System called "Dinner Party":

- Values—each guest has a set of Values that determine his or her meal preferences and seating.
- Policies—this might be the etiquette surrounding the use of cutlery.
- Events—these are the changes in state when, say, each dish arrives, or as people are seated.
- Content—this would be the menu and the conversations— possibly the reason for the party.
- Trust—this might be the Trust relationships between each of the guests, which would impact the quality and depth of their conversations. It might also be the collective relationship between the party guests and the cook/serving staff.

Using the five dimensions, we can describe the complete behavior of the 'Dinner Party Information System' and the desired outcomes of the host, all the guests, and those involved in delivery of supporting services (e.g. cooks and servers). In contrast, imagine if we tried to model the same party using process and data modeling tools and techniques, we would lose important facts—facts that affect the outcome. So, if it's hard to model the simple information system of a dinner party, what are the chances of modeling an entire corporation's information system without losing important facts? Preventing this loss of information is the aim of VPEC-T analysis.

We can look to the practice of asset management in manufacturing for a more business-focused scenario. Asset management is the practice of maintaining all the equipment in a facility and making sure that it performs a in way that increases return on investment and meets corporate goals. Here is a brief summary of the sort of issues a VPEC-T analysis would surface:

- Values
  Asset management staff is rewarded for avoiding unplanned outages, reducing maintenance costs, and performing maintenance on schedule. These Values require bringing equipment offline to maintain it, and are frequently in direct conflict with operations personnel, who run the equipment to create the products that are sold. The operations personnel want to keep the equipment running constantly to increase throughput. Building a solution for asset management that does not address the communication needed to resolve this conflict will result in the *automation of tension*, not productivity.

- Policies
  Asset management changes policy based on the position of the factory in the market. If the market is sold out, meaning that every product easily finds a buyer, then the Policy is to focus on keeping the equipment running, rather than reducing maintenance costs. In a market where the products are not sold out, the policy may be to reduce maintenance costs as much as possible. Any solution must be aware of these Policies and the ebb and flow between them.

- Events
  The work orders that maintenance technicians use to perform maintenance tasks or inspections are generated from a variety of sources. Scheduled maintenance based on the calendar or usage levels generates work orders. Systems that monitor the condition of equipment can generate work orders automatically. When a policy changes or a safety Event happens, every piece of equipment may need to be checked for a certain type of defect. If all of the Events are systematically searched for and identified, the resulting solution will be able to automate and process them efficiently and have the best chance of success.

- Content
  The work order is the key information dissemination and collection device for asset management. Information collected on the work order is used to create asset and maintenance histories, and to determine which parts are needed from inventory for a repair. A detailed understanding of the flow of Content to and from the work order can provide those implementing a solution with a complete context, so that as many needs as possible can be met.

- Trust
  Maintenance technicians frequently ask operations for a window of downtime to perform repairs. Operations staffers ask maintenance to skip the maintenance window so they can keep running. The information system supporting both of these activities must provide each conversation with the information needed, so that the decision about each request can be based on data, and not politics or local priorities. In order for the conversations about asset management to be effective, both sides must trust that the other is performing in the best interests of the larger organization, not just to meet their own selfish needs. An information system provides the data and support for collaboration needed to build Trust.

Conflicts and Change

The bulk of this book will explain VPEC-T, its implications, and how to apply it in greater detail. The explanation will be more effective, however, if we keep the following aspects of VPEC-T in mind.

The Search for Conflicts

As the dedicated reader will discover from the practitioner interviews at the end of this book, perhaps the biggest benefit of VPEC-T analysis is the identification of conflicts of various types and the attempt to resolve them sooner rather than later.

Conflicts in Values or Policies are a huge source of unclear or conflicting requirements. A systematic search for the way that two or more conflicting Values may come into play in an information system brings a sharp focus to the need for describing the correct behavior. Often the correct behavior cannot be described without first resolving the conflict in Values. VPEC-T analysis also frequently surfaces contradicting Policies. Frequently, these conflicts are easy to resolve, but sometimes they require effort on the part of senior staff in an organization. In any case, recognizing the conflicts avoids wasting time building solutions that lack clear direction about the correct behavior that should be supported.

Another cultural change that VPEC-T brings about is the direct acknowledgement of the result of past failures and poor communication in an organization. The echo of these failures is a nagging sense of distrust between all parties that works against progress of any kind. The first step forward is to acknowledge that this mistrust exists, and to understand that, if it goes unchecked, it will be

Fix It Before It's Broken

One of the central points of VPEC-T is the notion that conflicts in information system design must be dealt with and resolved in order to get the highest chance of meaningful results. The process of working through the dimensions of VPEC-T can sometimes surface conflicts in an organization that had previously been shoved under the carpet—this is a good thing! By bringing these conflicts to life and thinking about how they might be resolved, the tensions that would otherwise thwart adoption of the right IT solutions are dealt with in advance. This also gives the business an opportunity to resolve conflicts that may be affecting other aspects of the operation, outside of the specific information systems problem you are trying to solve—one of most subtle and powerful aspects of the VPEC-T technique.

a corrosive force. The second step is to use VPEC-T to achieve small victories that act to restore Trust. Eventually, in an environment of Trust, VPEC-T analysis speeds business transformation. In other words, Trust is efficient.

Adoption Engineering

While use of VPEC-T generally has a profound effect on the way business and IT work together to deliver the business change sought, the related practice of Adoption Engineering, which is covered in Chapter 5, is also proving to be powerful. Adoption Engineering is a family of approaches and frameworks and styles that focus on:

- *How IT solutions will be **adopted** by the users and other stakeholders.*
- *How to first clarify the desired **business outcomes** and then maintain focus on them.*

Adoption Engineering comprises a broad family of techniques— some of them well known, others less so. VPEC-T is part of the DNA in this family—it underpins many of the techniques in a way that combines business and IT—or to be more precise, in an Information Systems way. VPEC-T is the common language of Adoption Engineering.

While VPEC-T acts to turn the lights on and expand awareness, Adoption Engineering explains specific techniques and practices that act to promote focus on adoption of the solution.

VPEC-T as an Architectural Paradigm

When architecture practitioners are involved in doing a VPEC-T analysis, it frequently changes their thinking about the nature of architecture. With Values and Policies setting the framework and Trust as a key concern, architects frequently start thinking of systems in terms of Events and Content that are used by an information system but not owned by a particular application or database. This can move the architects (business, IT, and enterprise) in the direction of more loosely coupled, event-driven architectures, implemented using a system of services. The result is that the architectural constructs used by IT are abstracted out from the technology used to implement them. In other words, architects are infected by information systems thinking and tend to think of VPEC-T not only as a framework for analysis and requirements, but also as an "architectural style." The architects then search for re-usable patterns that include the VPEC-T dimensions.

VPEC-T and Externalization

Externalization is the underlying IS trend toward **ubiquitous information sharing and access to services**—where information and services are available to anyone or any machine, for any purpose. We see in the trend:

- *The breaking apart of the concepts of applications and databases to expose the business-meaningful parts of an Information System.*
- *Making tacit, human knowledge and behavior explicit.*
- *Integrating externally owned information sources and services of value to the Business Information System.*
- *Consuming and publishing business-meaningful events within and outside the enterprise.*

Externalization also invites management to consider whether there are existing services provided on the Web (such as Software-as-a-Service offerings like Salesforce.com or Google Apps) first, before they decide to implement services internally within the organization.

The simplifying, and technology-decoupling, nature of VPEC-T thinking supports this trend. The externalization of business and IT, which we discuss in greater detail in Chapter 5, is being achieved as

Information Systems and the Big Picture

Focusing on information systems involves focusing on the behavior of the people involved, their motivations, the way they interact, their core Values, and the Policies that implement those Values. Just as the scope of information systems is larger than the IT solutions, the Values and Policies unearthed in information systems design can be used on a larger scale still. In many of the organizations that have tried it, VPEC-T has been adopted as a de-facto architectural paradigm, because the V and P dimensions are applied not only to the system in question, but also to many systems outside the scope of the original project. The approach, in this way, has a regenerative effect on IS thinking throughout the organization, and it gets easier to re-apply as you go on. The beginning of the second VPEC-T analysis can start with the Values and Policies identified in the first. In this way, VPEC-T analysis becomes additive and represents an *architecture of behavior* that supersedes the project. Thinking about VPEC-T in a big-picture way seems to have many benefits.

the systems we use involve more and more collaboration, more and more use of systems provided by external sources, and more and more do-it-yourself functionality. As the *how* becomes more pliable, the *what* becomes more important. VPEC-T helps address what solutions should be doing, how they can meet their goals effectively, and how to manage risks in an externalized world.

Because the scope of VPEC-T is always larger than the scope of a single information system (vertical application), adopting VPEC-T as a philosophy is the beginning of creating a lasting and reusable understanding of the information systems in an organization. The rest of the book illuminates all the various aspects of information systems and their importance to the adoption of IT-enabled change.

VPEC-T: the Cartoon Version

Solutions out of Balance

Solutions created without proper input from the business side are inevitably driven by the concerns and fancies of the IT staff. *What* the solution should do to help the business is overcome by *how* the solution will be delivered.

The capabilities of existing IT infrastructure and applications, of vendor products such as enterprise business application software, or of services available over the Web (e.g., Software as a Service) determine the shape of the solution, not the business needs. The reason for this is that the business people lack a method and a language to capture the complexity of their requirements and express in business terms the details of what the solution must accommodate.

The result is that the solutions created are out of balance, as shown in Figure 1-3:

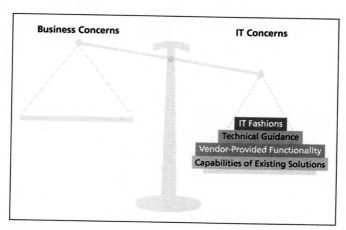

Figure 1-3: A Solution Out of Balance

A solution that is out of balance is one that creates a struggle for adoption. The business side does not find its needs met by the solution. Data must be entered, but everything seems like a lot of work for dubious value.

In the terms of our previous explanation, VPEC-T conquers the complexity that leads to this imbalance, and does so by supplying practitioners with information they can use, restoring balance.

The Result of VPEC-T: A Balanced Solution

The result of applying VPEC-T is a balanced solution as shown in Figure 1-4. The IT department's reasonable concerns are now matched, but a much larger body of knowledge about key issues that should inform the shape and functionality of a new solution now exists. Business and IT architects can design solutions—making use of (for example) existing applications and infrastructure, new business application software, new infrastructure products, and/or services available over the Web—with a better understanding of the behavior of the people involved, the goals they are trying to meet, and the way that information flows.

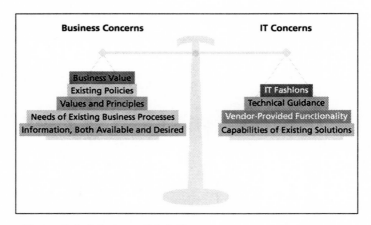

Figure 1-4: A Balanced Solution

The Benefits of VPEC-T

While VPEC-T is a new concept, it has been developed by the authors in several different engagements to develop solutions in environments that faced intractable challenges. A growing number of practitioners

---

Who should read this book?

- *Business Leaders who are curious about how "systems" work*
- *IT Leaders*
- *Change Practitioners (IT and Business)*

Our big request is that you occasionally put down the book and visualize applying VPEC-T to situations familiar to you.

"We'd like to think this book will find its way to the CIO's bookshelf—wedged firmly between *The Mythical Man-Month* and *The Tao of Pooh*".

—The Authors.

---

in a variety of industries are starting to report that VPEC-T has the following impact:

- Decreases the risk of IT project failure,
- Highlights the people and organizational issues associated with IT adoption,
- Increases opportunities for innovation,
- Highlights the opportunities for shared IT-enabled services,
- Informs IS/IT strategies and road maps.

Organizations have found the VPEC-T approach and output useful when considering:

- Highly Federated business situations (e.g., International Supply Chains),
- Balancing Central control with Local freedom-to-act,
- Reducing IT Time-to-Market barriers,
- Developing Shared Services and IT Commoditization (e.g., SaaS) strategies,
- Developing a business-system model to take advantage of Service-Oriented Architecture and Web 2.0 technologies,

- Developing Semantic-Web strategies and new information models that combine tacit and explicit information,
- Developing Event-based technology strategies (e.g., RFID and BAM),
- Developing Managed Service Provision business models (e.g., Supply Chain intermediaries or SaaS Providers),
- Developing "Change-ready" IT strategies,
- Developing post-M&A IS/IT strategies,
- Developing customizable services to their clients without perpetuating "point solutions,"
- Dealing with complex interacting Systems of Value (e.g., Governments),
- Dealing with complex information privacy and protection concerns.

Putting this Book to Work

 While VPEC-T is fun to read about and even more fun to write about, the real pleasure comes from putting the framework to work. The authors and other practitioners find that, in everyday conversations, they are much quicker to realize that a dispute is, at its core, about Values, or that the real problem is that Trust has never been established.

Systems thinking is useful in itself and has many advocates, and the authors encourage anyone with any interest to expand their knowledge in this area. (Check out the annotated bibliography for the authors' favorite books on the subject.) But you don't have to take a course on systems theory to use VPEC-T. The next time you are in a conversation about how to solve a problem, try to identify the Values and Policies in play. What Events are triggering action? What exactly is the Content being exchanged? Is Trust or the lack of it helping or hurting?

So, to put it simply, we believe that focusing on *information systems*, rather than "the business" or "IT," and accepting that people (and their behavior) and technologies play an equally important part in them, leads to a common understanding of what's needed, what isn't needed, and what will be adopted. Simple, really—and perhaps because it's so simple, you might hear a little voice say, "Why bother with the rest of the book?"

The answer is equally simple: we just want to explore our thinking, examples, and possibilities with you. We have one straightforward purpose in mind—to get you to try it for yourself. Perhaps even now, why not consider a part of your business you'd like to transform, and from the perspective of the key participants, write down a few words each about the V, P, E, C and T. Table 1-1: The VPEC-T Dimensions on page 10 will remind you of the straightforward definitions for each if you need it. Trying it out it might surprise you.

When you do try it for yourself, we do hope you drop us a line. We'd love your feedback on the book and on "thinking" and using VPEC-T in your professional life. Go to *www.LIThandbook.com*

Chapter 2

Information Systems Thinking: Examining What, Not How

It is possible to get tremendous value out of the VPEC-T framework just by focusing on the five words themselves and then using them to improve communication. The questions associated with each of the words are powerful: What Values and Policies are in play? What are the key Events and Content and the patterns in the way they are used? How is Trust helping or hurting and how can it be restored if need be? Most solution development projects would benefit from asking these questions early and often.

To get the most value from the VPEC-T framework, one must understand a bit more clearly how and why it works. VPEC-T delivers value primarily because it takes the focus off of information technology and directs focus on the information system. The information system describes the behavior of the people involved, their motivations, the interactions between people and different levels of the organization, and how information flows and changes.

The authors firmly believe that it is time to blow the dust off the whole idea of information systems and apply VPEC-T to information systems, so that you can better understand why IT projects are failing or are never implemented in the first place. In this chapter, we show how focusing on the VPEC-T dimensions helps by creating a better start point for the journey from specified IS to implemented IT. This chapter will explain the concept of information systems, but will also ask why approaches such as process modeling, IT architecture frameworks, and other approaches, while useful, fall short of capturing all the requirements of an information system.

What are Information Systems?

Advances in the capabilities, penetration and ambition of IT have made it more complex for businesses to understand, apply and manage. It seems that because IT can do so much more than before, it's getting harder to understand what it *can* do and harder for us to articulate what we *want* it to do. And the more advanced the solution, the more potentially complex its internal mechanisms. It has become common practice to change the way people work to match the needs of the technology. Such standardization has sometimes led to sensible improvements in business operations (such as deployments of software package applications or online application services), but this always requires a degree of conformity and consistency. Many IT users would say this hasn't always been appropriate or helpful from their point of view. Indeed, how can we decide which way is the right way for any given problem—do we fit IT-to-Process-to-People or People-to-Process-to-IT?

Information Technology pervades every aspect of our personal and business lives and it continues to get cheaper to do more complex things. In particular, new Web-based technologies are providing a mechanism through which people who do not want to *conform* to corporate norms do not have to conform. A dramatic example is Salesforce.com, the on-line sales-force application service provider. Its owners have found that their product is often first adopted by small groups of sales representatives, who then spread the word until the whole company adopts it—a bottom-up process of adoption.

So how can we hope to manage this growing muddle? How can we avoid making costly mistakes by selecting the wrong strategy? How can we understand which particular IT solution is going to be really useful and which is going to be useless?

To answer these questions, we need to stand back from the technology and think more clearly about how the business *Information System* should be operating, and only after that, consider IT possibilities. VPEC-T improves solution building processes because it forces a shift in this direction. Only with a full set of requirements that fills the VPEC-T gaps will we know how to choose from the IT possibilities and determine the IT solution which enables the *Information System* to work better, or faster, or cheaper, or, ideally, all three.

The Difference (and Relationship) between Information Systems and Information Technology

We have concluded that it's now time to take a renewed look at IS, and in doing so, perhaps surprisingly, we might find some answers to the challenges we see today associated with managing IT complexity and delivering more successful business outcomes. But to do this, we need to step back and consider the true nature of an Information System.

Many of us can recall a time when a distinction was made between the hardware and software supporting the business and the information used by the business—there was a clear difference between IT, to describe the former, and IS, to describe the latter.

IS stood for Information Systems, which might be described as:
The landscape of business information used by people within an organization and the way they use information to deliver business outcomes.

IT, in contrast, could be described as:
The hardware and software technology that automates or otherwise supports information processing.

This distinction has become lost, and the disciplines associated with IS (such as Business and Systems Analysis) have slipped from

Whatever happened to the Business Analyst?

The change in status of the IS disciplines was probably, in part, caused by the rise in enterprise software packages and the associated promise that business processes could be more easily automated, and efficiency gains realized, by simply buying an out-of-the-box solution. This was a powerful promise. It contrasted with the corporate experience of expensive, and often unsatisfying, custom-built software in conjunction with unsuccessful Business Process Engineering projects. ERP/CRM/MRP solutions were increasingly seen as being more business-relevant, and as a tool to implement standardization and efficiency across many business activities and user communities.

During this time, many Business Analysts transformed into package-configuration specialists and, in doing so, became more focused on the features and functions of the package than on business behavior. Others with expertise in IS gravitated to the world of IT architecture. This discipline, while often not seen as value-additive by the package proponents, was gaining respectability with large organizations that realized that packages needed to coexist with each other and the rest of the IT estate.

At the same time, the revolution in Open Source and Web technologies meant that the focus of architecture began to move away from the organization's Information Systems needs and closer to the Information Technology standards, tools and methods. The sheer complexity of all aspects of "architecture" meant that areas of technology-focused specialization began to develop within the architecture community.

prominence. Now included under the IT banner, the IS disciplines waned through lack of attention from the IT community and by lack of sponsorship by the business.

It's now time to resurrect the general concept of Information Systems, and take the opportunity to update the way we consider IS. Specifically, today's focus for IS business analysis should be on:

- Simplifying, negotiating, and consolidating requirements across all aspects of the business, but with the top-of-the-office business outcomes front-of-mind.

- Identifying repeating patterns of business activity and seeking out opportunities for shared competencies and services.
- Focusing on the behavioral aspects of the business that are proven to be barriers to adopting IT solutions. These include the hierarchies of personal and collective Value Systems and Trust relationships.
- Focusing on the elementary aspects of the business' Information System, such as rules and constraints embedded in Policies, the business-meaningful, real-world, events of interest, and the information content being exchanged between individuals and groups.
- Communicating the business "*what*" without reference to the technology "*how*."

As we pointed out in Chapter 1 and will emphasize for the rest of the book, shifting the focus as just described appears to provide a way to help conquer complexity. It simplifies the gathering of business requirements and helps restore business/IT balance.

Hard versus Soft Information Systems

There has been an historical misclassification of both the word "information" and the word "system." Here's the problem with the way the

Did Data Modeling help the dust gather on IS?

Many attempts have been made to develop Information Systems architecture using rigorous data-modeling techniques. While sophisticated, these were expensive, and often seemed to do no more than paper the walls with incomprehensible wiring diagrams. The apparent waste of time and money spent on such mega-modeling projects frustrated CxOs greatly and created a mistrust that blocked deeper analysis of Information Systems.

The IS architects, however, have always felt that their desire for semantic accuracy was misunderstood, and that the business was ignoring their rigorous models at its peril.

word "information" is used. Before computers as we know and use them today existed, engineers in radio and telegraph communications were concerned with measuring transmissions and their degree of distortion. The actual content of these signals—what was being said in the signal transmission—wasn't important to them. They were primarily concerned with maintaining the fidelity of the signal and were indifferent to the information being exchanged. As a result, what has historically been called "information systems" actually refers to the mechanistic functioning of technological components, not the business value or content of the information being conveyed via these components. The focus is on the "how" rather than the "what."

There is also a considerable semantic issue surrounding the word "system."

Traditional IT thinking is *systematic* in nature. Systematic refers to the idea that a process or methodology can be encapsulated or even replicated by a system. This way of thinking conceives of the world literally as a "Hard" system, and as having conditions that can be reproduced directly through technology. Systematic thinking has historically developed rigid projects that are inflexible; organizations often find it easier to change the business process to suit the technology solution than to make the technology match the business. The robotic tail wags the in-the-flesh dog.

Systemic thinking, or "soft systems methodology," is different. Systemic concerns a "system as a whole." The pedals on a bicycle are useful only when they are integrated with wheels, spokes, and chains into the bicycle as a whole. If one laid all of the parts of an unassembled bicycle on the ground and pointed to them, saying, "this is a bicycle," most rational people would disagree—these parts do not function as a coherent whole. Systemic thinking concerns a whole entity as having "emergent properties" and a "layered structure and processes of communication and control, which in principle allow it to survive in a changing environment."

When we use "soft systems methodology" and look at our organizations *systemically*, as opposed to a "hard systems" approach

> ### Source: Wikipedia
>
> **Systems theory** is an <u>interdisciplinary</u> field of <u>science</u>. It studies the nature of <u>complex systems</u> in <u>nature</u>, <u>society</u>, and <u>science</u>. More specifically, it is a framework by which one can analyze and/or describe any group of objects that work in concert to produce some result. This could be a single organism, any organization or society, or any electro-mechanical or informational artifact. While systems concepts had long been used in sociology and the area is often associated with <u>cybernetics</u>, systems theory as a technical and general academic area of study predominantly refers to the science of systems that resulted from <u>Bertalanffy's</u> General System Theory (GST), among others, in initiating what became a project of systems research and practice. It was <u>Margaret Mead</u> and <u>Gregory Bateson</u> that developed interdisciplinary perspectives in systems theory (such as positive and negative feedback in the social sciences).
>
> Systems theory can be helpful when we want to consider the potential of emergent technologies, such as those emerging from Web 2.0/3.0 trends, and the impact on the future direction of corporate IT. It helps us look at both the softer, interactive and harder, transactive aspects of an overall information system.

(systematically), the bicycle not only functions as a whole and moves forward when we push the pedals; it also swerves to avoid potholes and stops for crossing ducklings. It adapts, changes, and absorbs shocks, just like organizations and individual humans do.

It is critical to understand the importance of human behavior, social norms and planned and unplanned events to information systems. These aspects, if left unexplored, often become the barriers to adoption of IT-enabled change. For better-faster-cheaper IT, we need to seek out the sweet spot between classical, "hard" engineering approaches and the early examination of "softer" adoption barriers. Some of the most successful Web-enabled businesses (such as Google, Amazon, and eBay) have used an adoption-led, "soft" approach to the development of products and services. By "adoption-led," we mean an experiential approach that focuses on how products and services are adopted by the market and respond to those patterns—building on successes and dropping failures. Corporate IT, in contrast, often continues to take a more traditional, "hard" approach to engineering the way to a solution.

In a sense, VPEC-T seems to confirm the message of the so-called "agile development methodologies." At its core, agile methods are based on the proposition that there is a huge payoff for being suspicious of the requirements for a project. In reaction to that suspicion, agile methods focus on building the smallest usable portion of a system and then rapidly improving it in a set of incremental steps. VPEC-T has a similar recommendation to the practice of requirements gathering. VPEC-T is based on the proposition that there is a huge payoff for delaying the focus on IT implementation issues, instead focusing on the nature of the information system at the center of the solution being considered. In a sense, both VPEC-T and agile methods recommend waiting and getting experience rather than rushing into building a complete solution.

The Search for Conflicting Values

Now that we've explained what we mean by information systems, we can now show you how VPEC-T incorporates some of these principles, as well as the potential traps along the way to adoption-led engineering.

Information Systems: The Collective Persona

Alan Cooper, inventor of Visual Basic and pioneer of interaction design, invented the Persona as a way to improve the process of designing user interfaces. Personae are descriptions of hypothetical people who would use the interfaces being designed. Those people would be given names and they would have personal details, even caricatures and photos, ascribed to them. This allowed

UI designers to make decisions about UI elements that would in theory make the "Personae" happier and more productive. Using VPEC-T to gather requirements in solution-building plays the same role as do Personae in UI design. VPEC-T acts as a meta-persona, or Collective Persona, that describes the personality and behavior of all of the people who are going to use the information system. It is this Persona, when deployed, which provides the more esoteric information that had been missing and restores value to the solution-building or configuration process. If the Collective Persona is communicated during VPEC-T analysis, then you can make decisions about ideas that can be used to make information systems, just as UI designers did with Personae. This averts uncomfortable situations, where the IT head comes and asks the business side about some technical detail that the business side doesn't know the impact of. The IT staff can make more decisions on their own, and make them correctly with the VPEC-T analysis in hand, because it acts as a Collective Persona and allows the IT department to answer a lot of those questions on their own.

One of the most important aspects of VPEC-T is its focus on searching for the values in play in an information system and attempting to identify conflicts as early as possible.

Many business leaders adopt a value-based approach to turning a concept into action within their businesses. Their approach is designed to motivate people to act differently, to define new processes, and to use IT to deliver the business result—turning concept into action.

It's been long recognized that there is a *loss in translation* during this concept-to-action process. This is the noise created between the desired outcome of the board and the IT solution the Users receive to support it. (See Figure 2-1, "The Swing." This picture was originally drawn back in the 1980s or earlier.) Somewhere along the line, the values articulated by the business still get lost today, despite the valiant efforts and best practices of IT practitioners.

Figure 2-1: "The Swing"

What is the role of Value Systems in solution building?

We have borrowed the term Value System from philosophy (see Pirsig reference in the bibliography). In the context of business and the people within it, a Value System is a set of values of a person or a group or an organization (e.g., the employee, the department or the company). Each individual, group, or organization will have its own unique Value System. The use of the word "system" here implies a complex set of relationships between various values, some of which may conflict with others—e.g., Ethics, versus a desire for wealth or a desire for strategic change, versus short-term shareholder value. The business outcome-relevant aspects of personal and corporate Value Systems must be aligned to convert a top-down concept to action and delivered results.

So why should we pay more attention to Value Systems, in IT projects?

Explicit recognition of the Value Systems within the scope of the project provides additional, and often missing, context for process change and IT design. Identifying the values that are in play and resolving any conflicts helps to prevent desired business outcomes from being lost in translation on the journey to IT solution design. It helps the designers provide IT to Users that also works for them. It does so by understanding the relevant values of the all the participants and the relationships between them. Simply, this makes the IT solution easier for the Users to adopt, thereby shortening *concept-to-action* time. When value conflicts are left unresolved, the project frequently becomes a forum for airing conflicts, which inhibits progress and destroys trust.

The Problem with Process

The marriage of users and IT is a vital union, but it is beset by awkwardness and poor communication. When specifying require-ments of a proposed IT solution, the language of users can differ significantly from the language of the IT specialist. This difference in language is a reflection of apparently opposing values (or Value Systems) in play. Fundamentally, the users want a system that works the way they do, which is often amenable to change and supports learning. The IT specialist, on the other hand, seeks a high degree of functional certainty and actionable rules that can be configured or encoded.

To support business-efficiency goals, many envisage the world as a set of neatly ordered, well-planned, pre-determined and sequenced set of activities—just as Henry Ford did when he introduced the production line. This is hardly surprising, as it is a tried-and-tested approach to manufacturing, and more generally reflects a simple, intelligent goal—to be more efficient at a task through understanding and optimizing all the steps involved. However, optimization and automation require all the steps and parties involved to be specifically defined, so this approach usually seeks to "decompose" the task into detailed models of all the interacting parts within the "end-to-end" process.

This method can often work well with discrete operations, but its weaknesses are exposed when the process in question spans departmental or external boundaries. This is apparent to organizations that are finding their business processes to be increasingly diverse, dispersed, and complex. Ownership of the end-to-end process is often unclear and the process isn't understood in its entirety. To make matters worse, requirements analysis is focused on the *specific functional needs* of a particular user community. This often creates tension between, for example, a corporate desire for greater standardization, and the User desire for functional fit.

For example, a corporation, for sake of efficiency and economy, may wish to deploy a single interface into its accounting system that will look the same to all employees. But this goal might not consider the need to customize screen organization for the many geographies the company operates in, nor the many reasons employees may need to log into the accounting system—sales and service have very different financial organizations, and their IT should reflect that. This is caused by a narrow focus on the minutia of the work-task and functional specification of such. In short, this approach can make the analysis increasingly complex, and the desired corporate-level outcomes more elusive. But perhaps the most critical failure of this focus—on steps, tasks, and procedures, that is, *hard* systems—is in its poor representation of the softer, more knotty problems associated with differing/conflicting business values, policies, operational "realities," and governance models.

Common ground must be found between these seemingly opposing values of hard and soft systems so that the marriage will work.

Out of necessity the language of users embraces:	Out of necessity the language of the IT function embraces:
The ambiguous	High-specification
Market forces and complex societal issues	Certainty
Tacit knowledge and behavior based on constant learning	Explicit knowledge and behavior based on pre-determined rules
High-change	Low-change

Table 2-1: User language and IT Language Compared

To make matters worse, the gaps and inconsistency in the business requirements often forces the IT engineer to attempt to complete the picture. IT engineering relies upon techniques and tools that are designed to convert process and policy—not the softer issues—into precise rules and constraints. This focus results in unresolved differences in values between users, trust issues, and perhaps most importantly, unresolved conflicts or "tension points" that determine the behavior of the Information System, or prevent the IT solution from being adopted at all.

The dialog between user and the IT specialist becomes focused on the detailed features, functions and volumetric aspects of the proposed IT solution. And the desired business outcomes of the sponsoring executive (Business Stakeholder) become obscured by this drive for detail, and led by the Users' individual and collective desires. In other words, the big picture gets lost because of the focus on the details of IT implementation—neither the User nor the IT specialist can see the forest for the trees.

Standardization of Behavior

Attempts to solve this problem often result in the Business Stakeholder issuing standardization edicts to the Users and the IT specialists, in

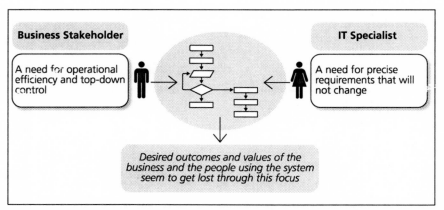

Figure 2-2: Collusion between the Business Stakeholder and the IT Specialist

an attempt to ensure that operational efficiency goals are met and key business outcomes are delivered. This can result in an unwitting collusion between the Business Stakeholder and the IT specialist, based on a top-down "design" of the business processes—this is a so-called "design," without a sufficiently detailed understanding of the business operation. Both parties are driven by a desire to build standardized behavior into the IT solution.

The Business Stakeholder wants efficiency and control and the IT specialist wants formalism and specification. While this approach has been proven to work in the past, particularly for highly predictable business activities, many businesses are seeking flexibility and agility in their core processes—these goals require different thinking. Traditional IT is transactional and secure, emphasizing reliability and scalability. New forms of IT are more flexible and user-driven, emphasizing collaboration and flexibility. The top-down edict approach to driving IT-enabled business change projects often creates four major problems:

- **Adoption Barriers**—the users are less inclined to adopt the IT solution, claiming that it doesn't work for them—they continue to use and develop Shadow IT solutions.

- **Brittle Processes**—the top-down specification of "process" works against flexibility and becomes a barrier to future business change.
- **Business/IT Misalignment**—the organizational and management models of the business are not properly reflected in the IT solution. For example, in a multinational business with diverse operations, it may be necessary and desirable to allow a high degree of local freedom-to-act, in, say, local sales processes.
- **Shadow IT**—users begin creating "work-arounds" that bypass the rigid systems, using the new, flexible technologies, such as Web 2.0 and instant messaging, thus subverting the whole purpose of, for example, an expensive ERP installation.

Flexible IT and the Diamond Model

It seems we need a different approach to specify requirements for IT: an approach that balances the desired business outcomes of the stakeholder with the needs of the user and delivers the precision needed by the IT specialist. This allows us to express what IT solutions can really do for the business.

Again, our use of language and a premature focus on IT are at the root of this problem. The language problem starts with how we express the concept of processes. The word *"process"* can have very different meanings and implications. These can range from the loose collection of unsystematic activities that support a Contract Negotiation or HR process, to the highly repetitious and predictable behavior of a production line. What we believe is needed is a common language for describing the range of business behavior across this continuum.

A premature focus on IT drives the analysis of the business problem toward IT engineering approaches, which obscures other outcome-affecting aspects. To make matters worse, IT engineering methods and techniques are designed to drive completeness and precision for

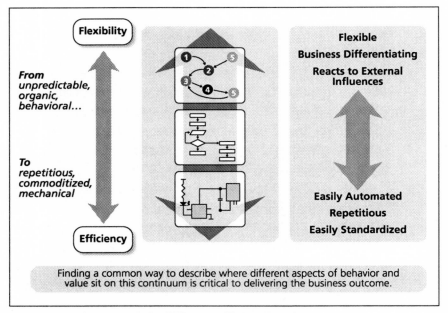

Finding a common way to describe where different aspects of behavior and value sit on this continuum is critical to delivering the business outcome.

Figure: 2-3: The Process Flexibility to Efficiency Scale

systems, and in doing so, introduce a language that is, by its nature, hard for the business to understand. This can result in frustration on both sides of the Business/IT divide, with neither party understanding the needs of the other.

This premature focus on IT severely stymies innovation and flexibility. The sheer volume of information produced during the engineering lifecycle means the overall business context gets lost in the production of wiring diagrams and technical schema. The complexity of the task requires a high degree of specialized technical knowledge that can lead to a lack of focus on the nuances of real-world behavior and human interaction "on the ground." Often the focus is slanted toward the engineering *"How"* rather than the business *"What"*—i.e., the intended business outcome.

The reality is that many business scenarios are more organic and unpredictable than pre-determinable and mechanistic. Further, in today's connected world, many business scenarios encounter tensions—between corporate and local functions, between customers and suppliers, and between partners. No one is in control of the end-to-end processes, rather, a combination of interacting service agreements make up the overall value delivered to the customer.

Many of the threads of interaction that comprise a business work very well without formal "Process" definition. They are often based on unwritten conventions and are managed through the organization's structure. These types of processes are not top-down "designed." Think of them as flexible channels of activity that reflect the reality of the day-to-day operation—reacting to events as they happen. This is the world that VPEC-T captures. The processes are not mechanistic or standardized, but they are effective nonetheless. The people on the ground are simply good at getting the job done within the parameters set by their bosses. People will often make things work despite unhelpful, centrally defined and mandated processes, procedures, and IT systems.

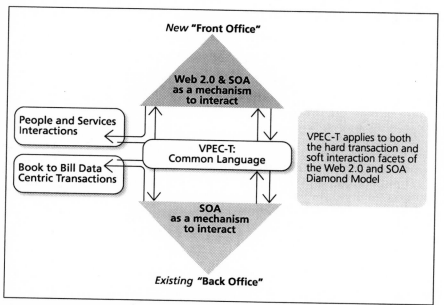

Figure 2-4: The Web 2.0 & SOA Diamond Model
(Reference *Mashup Corporations* by Andy Mulholland, et al)

Using VPEC-T does not supplant today's dominant techniques in IT—standardization and automation. It just supplies enough information so that IT and Business Process practitioners can get the best from those techniques. At times processes need to be mechanized and the functions of an enterprise are valuably served by an industrialized approach. At other times, the software should simply capture the content, raise events, enforce policies, and leave the people using the IT to complete the flow of information. This more flexible and less dogmatic approach better reflects real-world business collaboration and community participation.

The Role of Other Frameworks

There are well-known frameworks to aid business analysis and decision-making. Such frameworks are used as tools to derive desired business outcomes. Examples include Force Field, PEST, and SWOT analysis (the one compared to VPEC-T in the first chapter). Another set of frameworks exists that guides design of enterprise architecture for IT, specific examples include; the Integrated Architecture Framework (IAF), The Open Group Architecture Framework (TOGAF), and the Zachman framework. These two types of frameworks differ from each other in some important ways:

"Thinking" Frameworks	*"IT" Frameworks*
Aids decision-making relevant to achieving objectives	Specifies design of solutions and records the decisions made
Easy to understand and work with, can be picked up very quickly and used	Specialized and used by experienced practitioners
"Discovery of insight"	"Governance of IT"

Table 2-2: Frameworks

The lack of a business-friendly "thinking framework" for Information Systems, that is, the position occupied by VPEC-T, has been filled by IT frameworks, eagerly proposed by the IT practitioners. This doesn't work, because unlike the VPEC-T framework, IT frameworks are primarily focused on architecture and engineering. VPEC-T is focused on the communication of business concepts to all involved. On the surface, IT frameworks can appear appropriate—they often refer to business-meaningful concepts, such as Information, Process, Time, and Motivation dimensions, but their objectives are different, and the models developed often lack the ability to express VPEC-T. As a result, they can prove unhelpful when it comes to creating a common understanding of the VPEC-T dimensions.

To be clear, IT frameworks are important but they don't currently provide the complete answer. Such frameworks also make a distinction between IS and IT and promote abstraction up through layers from technology to business strategy, but they lack full expression of the VPEC-T dimensions. The authors strongly believe IT architecture and the associated frameworks are critical to successful and sustainable IT.

The lessons of this discussion are varied but clear. VPEC-T plays an important role in providing information, so that other techniques, such as process modeling and IT frameworks, can be applied with a deeper understanding. To meet many of the requirements that VPEC-T is likely to surface, it is likely that IT *itself* will have to change from a mechanistic, standardized form to one that is more flexible and allows users more room to collaborate. Keeping these points in mind will help avoid traveling down the off-ramps on the path to getting the full benefit of VPEC-T. In the next chapter, we dive deeply into each dimension of VPEC-T.

Chapter 3

VPEC-T in Detail: A Common Language Explained

Do it Now! Begin at Once!

The most important thing you can do to learn VPEC-T is try it out. You don't have to wait until you are building an IT system. Start with a family issue or a conflict at work. Think about the dimensions of VPEC-T and you might be surprised how often you'll find the hidden forces at play. (In everyday life, it seems that Values are at conflict much more often than we normally realize.)

Once you develop the habit of applying VPEC-T, especially if you do so formally when building an IT-based solution, you will start to wonder how this technique works. In fact, understanding how VPEC-T works does improve the value you get from it.

This chapter provides a step-by-step analysis of what happens when you apply each dimension of VPEC-T to a problem. Table 3-1 summarizes the benefits of VPEC-T. The rightmost column describes the benefits of using each dimension of VPEC-T.

	How it helps describe the Information System	How it helps provide guidance to the IT provider	The benefit of using this concept
Values	Identifies the important principles and goals in play, allowing conflicts that may cause confusion to be identified and resolved.	Ensures the solution supports the full landscape of Values (Value Systems).	Conflicts are resolved upfront. The solution created is better aligned with business practices and the desired business outcome.
Policies	Identifies specific practices and guidelines that the system must adhere to, allowing conflicts to be identified and resolved.	Ensures the solution supports the full landscape of specific Policies and guidelines.	Conflicts are resolved upfront and requirements for compliance with Policies are known throughout the solution-building process. The solution created is better aligned with business practices. Tight association and traceability from real-world policy to implemented rule in the IT solution.
Events	Identifies the trigger points that indicate the change in state of processes or otherwise important milestones.	Uses these trigger points not only to control the behavior of the solution being built, but as integration points with other systems.	Creates IT solutions that maximize the potential to reuse and repurpose Event information. Creates opportunities to use Event information for audit and business reporting. Creates opportunities to use Event information for integration, internally and externally. Allows implementation of multi-channel solutions. Maximizes the potential of a Service Oriented approach.

Content	The core content of the information system is clearly identified and put in context of the desired business outcome. It is represented in a way that is familiar to the business and treated in a consistent way, regardless of the communication channel/ medium or originating or receiving domain.	Clearly defines all the important content within the information system. IT solutions handle internal and external information exchange and integration in a more consistent manner.	All the Content used to support a desired business outcome is formally described within the information system (not just that held in corporate databases). This results in better application of IT. All relevant information exchanges are recorded both internally and externally.
Trust	Existing areas of mistrust are identified and addressed. Opportunities to build trust are searched for. Trust relationship risks are identified.	Business and IT both recognize Trust as a critical, outcome-affecting dimension and they actively build and protect Trust. Regulatory control needs and other risks associated with Trust relationships are made explicit.	As Trust grows, the solution design and delivery is more efficient and rewarding. Threats to Trust are dealt with directly. Barriers to the adoption of the IT solution are removed. Trust risks associated with regulatory control are built into the solution.

Table 3-1: VPEC-T Descriptions and Benefits

The Importance of Values

In Chapter 2, we talked about the importance of identifying conflicts in Value Systems and hinted at the importance of Values (of a person and of a community) in the context of an Information System and, by inference, to the Information Technology that supports it.

Understanding the Values of the people and organizations involved is critical to the adoption of IT solutions. These Values exist within the context of a particular business mission. These might be the Values of a particular line of business, the customer, the supplier, the employees or another party.

> There are two important aspects to "Values": goals and beliefs. Goals tend to be transient—for example, a profit margin or customer-retention outcome in a financial year. Beliefs tend to constrain and enable the way a goal is achieved.

These Values are not visible in static workflows or other maps of processes that describe steps in a linear sequence. What is needed is a model that allows us to picture the interactions between Value Systems. Picture for a moment your organization as being composed of "threads of interaction" that cross, join, and otherwise interact. Think of "thread" as a set of steps that carry some task from beginning to end. These threads exist to deliver a specific business outcome. This could be, for example, the outcome associated with a Line-of-Business or Product/Service Operation. Now consider how that thread is influenced by a variety of Value Systems as it crosses departmental boundaries, geographies, and trading partnerships, and then as it traverses management hierarchies.

Think about the Value Systems of these stakeholders:

- The staff that undertake activities within processes
- The management teams
- The business partners
- The shareholders

All have a significant effect on business behavior. Business behavior is a critical aspect of an Information System, and resistance to changing this behavior is one of the most significant barriers to the adoption of IT solutions.

Let's look at a couple of examples:

- The Values (beliefs) of the Police are centered on *speed*— catching the bad guys quickly. However, the beliefs of the Prosecution agency are centered on *accuracy*—making sure only the guilty are sent to jail. Both of these Value Systems exist in their own right, but they also exist under the Value System of a nation's Justice Department, which might, for example, be focused on the goals of "improved victim and witness care." It's clear that these differing Values create tensions between the differing desired outcomes at the individual and group levels.
- The Values of the operations department of a factory are usually oriented toward throughput. Each shift wants to get as much product out the door as possible. Sometimes one shift doesn't really worry that putting off maintenance will cause delays, as long as the breakdown doesn't happen on their shift. The maintenance staffers want to perform scheduled maintenance to avoid having equipment break and halt production. For this reason, sometimes maintenance asks for a shutdown of normally scheduled production. If this conflict in Values is not resolved, a plant lurches from one sub-optimal state to another, from too many maintenance windows to too few. This conflict in Values is frequently only resolved by aligning the motivations of each side, that is, rewarding maintenance not just on performing scheduled maintenance but also on uptime. Or by rewarding production, not just on throughput but on avoidance of unplanned outages.

Values in IT Solutions

An IT solution that ignores differing Values is likely to be unpopular at best, or not implemented at worst. Of course, businesses are well aware that different Values apply across differing lines of business. But perhaps what is less obvious is the tension between user and community Values and those of the corporation or controlling body, and the effects of those tensions on corporate IT.

It's interesting to note here that we often discuss the Business/IT divide (the differing Values of business and those of an IT function), but here we're calling out a new "divide" between The Users and Corporate Governance.

Just as a common language must be established and a balance must be struck between business leaders and IT managers, corporate users and business leaders, who design corporate governance Policies, must find common ground and align their Values in order to continue to operate the business at optimum levels. Again, business leaders intuitively understand such differences, and successful leaders know

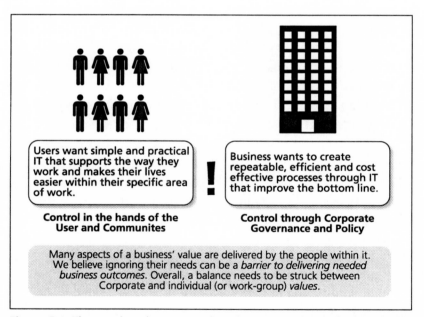

Figure 3-1: The tensions between what the user wants and what the enterprise wants

how to align staff around a common business vision and motivate them to execute accordingly. However, there appears to be a more subtle, less visible manifestation of this divide. Often this is seen, over-simplistically, as an IT problem—let's examine this further.

Users want simple and practical IT that supports the way they work and makes their lives easier within their specific area of work. Business, however, wants to create repeatable, efficient, and cost-effective processes through IT that improve the bottom line. This tension has been made more acute by the information technologies available to the user, through search services such as Google, Web communities such as Wikis, and mobile personal devices. These technologies are often personally owned and/or readily accessible. This is fuelling the development of more sophisticated "Shadow IT" (see Chapter 5) that sits outside the boundaries of corporate governance.

It might seem obvious to say: "business value is delivered by the people within,"—but it's common to see personal and collective Values of workgroups being ignored. This creates a barrier to delivering much-needed business outcomes. This is because people must adopt the higher business Values to realize the outcome, and they're unwilling to do this if it conflicts with their personal or departmental Values. To make matters worse, this is often at odds with their reward systems, because conflicting Value Systems have not been properly examined and aligned. For example, one way of resolving the conflict between production and maintenance in a factory is to put both functions in one department that is rewarded based on combined performance metrics. Overall, a balance needs to be struck between "corporate" and "user" Values by first recognizing their existence, and secondly, taking action to resolve, or otherwise manage, the tension points.

Today's Business/IT modeling and analysis approaches, however, don't focus on making Values explicit. They are often completely missing from the requirements and are obscured or ignored in the solution design.

Key questions to ask about Values:

- What are the Values of each participant?
- How are they aligned?
- How are they in conflict?
- What Values are in play at each level of organization—that is, for the individual, department, division, company, market, ecosystem, and economy at large?

Personae in Action

By answering these questions about Values, those building an IT solution are armed not just with information about potential conflicts, but also with general principles they can use to make technical decisions that would not be easy to explain to the business staff. For example, if flexibility is a key value, then it may make sense to construct a solution out of Web services that can be easily recombined, rather than building the solution in a less-flexible manner. The value of flexibility is that it crosses the IT boundary without forcing the IT staff to ask the business side if they want to "do this in Web services," a question that the business side wouldn't know how to answer.

This uncovered Value is an aspect of Persona.

Policies, Events and Content: the Core of an Information System

Just imagine for a moment that IT as we know it didn't exist. What language would we use to describe the information we need to run the business?

For simplicity, let's break the business Information System down into three primary chunks:

- **Policies**—The broad range of mandates and agreements such as internal Policies, Law, and external Contracts that apply across various parts of the business. These are the rules that govern and constrain how things get done.
- **Events**—The real-world proceedings that stimulate business activity—sometimes in a predefined sequence, but often not. These are the triggers for action.
- **Content**—The documents, conversations, or messages that are produced and consumed by business activities. These are the dialogues we use to share a plan, a concept, a history and/or the details of a person, place or thing.

These are of course the P-E-C dimensions of the VPEC-T framework. In fact, the framework started life with only these three dimensions—the V and the T were added later when we realized something was missing. However, we found that the Policies, Events, and Content core dimensions provide a convincing taxonomy root for describing a more traditional view of an Information System (without considering Values and Trust).

Interestingly, we find the more technically minded gravitate toward P-E-C and specifically the Events dimension. Focusing on Events first seems particularly helpful to architects working on complex integration. In fact, a number of our colleagues have developed an Architectural Style based on VPEC-T, with Events centricity in mind (this may be the subject of a future book).

Policies

The Policies dimension is used to focus thinking on the broad range of governing rules that constrain an activity. We use the term Policies to cover anything that sets a governance framework around the work being carried out, such as a corporate policy, a contract, a job description, a standard operating procedure or a departmental edict (written or verbal). There is a close, but often implicit, relationship between Policies and Values. However, these are often misaligned, which can create outcome-affecting tensions. It is also evident that, in some cases, one Policy may conflict with another. Policies also have different scope; some are broader than others. A prohibition on accepting gifts from clients is a broad policy covering lots of different behavior. A ban on first-class travel is a narrower policy. The choice to only use Avis for renting cars is even more specific.

Values and Policies

Imagine that an organization decides to set a goal to reduce the cost of IT—this goal is now part of its value system. The value, however, is not realizable until it is converted into Policy. The Policy in this case might, for example, be the contract and supporting Service Level Agreement with an IT Outsourcing provider.

Google's famous one-liner about its corporate Values is simple and memorable: "Don't be evil." This is a high-level Value that translates into many different sorts of Policies that support its brand in the market and make the company fun to work at. Values are rules without context. Policies, however, are rules that *provide* context, and realize Values. Policies and Values are close bedfellows, in that they provide guidance for behavior; however, a Value cannot be readily converted into a rule for an information system, which is why we identify Policy separately.

Policies created to share information may be in direct conflict with Data Privacy & Protection Policies. Lower-level Policies, such as Job Descriptions or Contracts may be misaligned with a high-level, mission-defining Policy, such as the Customer Service Charter, from the perspective of performance measurement and reward. Again, similar to Values, the tensions created should be addressed, if not completely resolved, before IT solutions are considered.

In some cases, through the use of VPEC-T, an issue of misalignment in a fundamental corporate governance policy could be identified. In this case, it may be necessary to create the opportunity to have a discussion with very senior business stakeholders before continuing with the IS/IT project. This conversation might be difficult to arrange and challenging to have. But if you are able to make a clear explanation of the issues and recommend steps towards its resolution and make it clear that a costly mistake has been avoided, you could be a hero!

The problem is that this alignment work is often missing from IT-enabled change programs, which results in adoption barriers and missed business outcomes. And, when we look under the hood of the IT world, we see that the link between Policies and logic-based rules (e.g., lines of programming code or configured rules) within IT solutions is obscured by language translations, and therefore hard to manage across the business/IT boundary.

Simply, Policies need to be aligned with corporate/group Values. They must set the constraining rules for information processing without loss of business meaning. Similarly to the analysis of Values, the risk of IT project failure is significantly reduced if the Policies in play are documented along with any tension points, in a way that's clear to all.

Key questions about Policies:

- What Policies are relevant to the information system being analyzed?
- What informal customs and practices are effectively Policies?
- Are any of the Policies in conflict with other Policies?
- Do the current Policies support current Values?
- Is there a need to set new Policies for areas of confusion about the correct behavior?

By focusing on clearly defining the Policies in play, the IT staff can better design the processes of a solution to accommodate them. Opportunities to change Policies that may result in process inefficiencies can also be identified.

The Scope of Values and Polices

VPEC-T maps the terrain of a much larger space than just the domain of one IT application. To put it another way, any specific business domain's information system is part of a larger context, and VPEC-T describes that context at the highest level, especially with respect to Values and Policies. As such, VPEC-T outputs are reusable. The analysis of a new information system may begin by collecting the Values and Policies from all previous VPEC-T analyses, and then starting to identify Values or Policies that are missing. Events and Content can also be shared between information systems (it's worth noting here that the externalization of Event information from "owning applications" is a growing trend). Trust is at play everywhere, and, like Policies and Values, may affect an entire organization.

Events and Content: Making a Clear Distinction between Events and Content

In order to explain the Events and Content dimensions, it is necessary to explain the difference between them and the importance of this, often under-represented, distinction. One of the most important outcomes of using VPEC-T for analysis is the resulting distinction between business Content and business Events.

Business Events (or more accurately, the IT representation of them) can be used in many ways, but their primary purpose is to provide actionable information (business signals) about the real-world proceedings within a business process. They are a simple, point-in-time "checkpoint" that helps us understand the progress toward a desired business outcome (e.g., shipment delivered, or payment received).

In the past, this information was typically internalized within a vertically focused software application, and often recorded for internal consumption by that application. Furthermore, the concept of "Events" was often left ill-defined or implicit.

This thinking might assume that, for example, the existence of a document (a type of Content), such as a Purchase Order, was evidence that an order was placed, and perhaps, the more dangerous assumption, that the Order was being progressed. This can create a problem if, for example, the data-capture (Content) activity is not actually synchronized with other activities (and their Events) associated with a business process.

The shipment-movement system of a logistics business provides an example. The electronic capture of a Waybill (Content) and its relationship to the tracking "checkpoints" (Events) highlights the need to recognize the Events of "Pick-Up Request" (which happens before the Waybill has been filled out), "Package Picked Up" (this Event might be captured before the electronic Waybill exists in the IT system) and the Event of "Package Received at Outbound Depot" (which tells us the package is on the move). In this example, the Waybill information is captured from a paper copy of a document several hours after the shipment was picked up, and so doesn't actually represent the movement of the shipment. It cannot be used as a proxy for the real-world Events along the "customer-request-to-shipment-delivery" timeline. This may seem obvious, but experience tells us that these important subtleties can and do get lost in IT solution designs.

If Events are recorded as snapshots of what actually happened, they provide visibility of the changes in state of a business process or processes. They can also provide an audit trail of business processes. This is particularly useful for businesses that need such information to meet regulatory requirements or otherwise want to track business activity on the ground.

The Content dimension, on the other hand, is used to describe the broader informational aspects of a dialog between one activity and another. This provides a heading under which business documents such as Orders, Lists, Plans, and Results are described. It also allows for other important outcome-affecting dialogs, such as human conversations, and the use of external reference information, to be captured as part of the business analysis.

Why is it so important to maintain the conceptual distinction between Events and Content? The simple answer is: because the concept of an Event often gets lost during the design of an information system

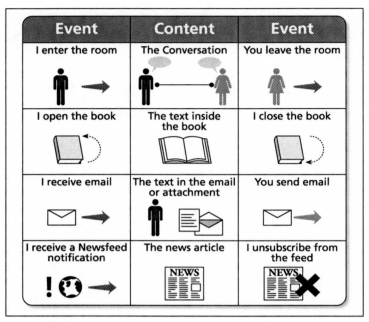

Figure 3-2: The distinction between Events and Content

and is then not available for further processing. This causes a further opportunity for confusion, as they are converted to programming code, configured rules, database elements, and stored procedures.

Most importantly, the business outcome can suffer (as described in the logistics example) from the resulting lack of distinction. Simply, protecting this distinction allows the analyst to ask business-relevant questions, such as:

What happened/is happening/will happen?
Versus
What do I want to know or say or ask or otherwise exchange?

It seems that most IT people are quite comfortable with Content-based discussions, often with the mental model of a database—or for the slightly more up-to-date, an XML structure—in mind. What usually happens is that the concept of the Event is missing from requirements discussions.

Key questions to ask about Content:

- What facts need to be known to achieve the desired outcome?
- What are the sources of information?
- How is that information currently gathered? Is it by asking someone face-to-face, via email, via an application, via the Web, etc.?
- What is the *context* of the information? How does the person using it understand it? Is there a "soft" context that implies meaning? For example, what is the time of day received or the Trust relationship with the information provider?

The Case for Event-centricity

Understanding Events as discrete items in an Information System also increases the possibility of re-use and re-purposing of the Events information. This "Externalization" of Events from within vertically focused databases and applications is discussed further in a later chapter. (See also Externalization and Adoption Engineering.)

How does an Event focus help early adoption and speed tangible business benefit?

Organizations that have adopted an Events-based approach are seeing seemingly subtle, but important, benefits:

- **Incremental Improvement**—This is the benefit associated with not needing to know all of the "Events of interest" upfront. It stems from having a standardized way of processing and recording Events and the "open" nature of an Event-based architecture. For example, it may not be possible to establish all the important Events associated with a complex business process ahead of time; even if they

---

Why is it useful to make Events "external"?

(That is, pull them out of a specific software application or database)

There are a number of arguments for doing this—but let's focus on a few key reasons for externalization of Events:

- **Business Federations**—In "federated" business situations, where many parties want to share Events across a broad range of IT systems and processes that span business domains such as a supply chain or a group of autonomous government departments.

- **IT Federations**—In a component-based or "Service Oriented" architecture, where multiple IT components may produce (to trigger another service) or consume Events (either used to trigger that service or to be processed by that service in order to construct new information by aggregating a number of business Events, for example).

- **Business Intelligence**—When a business can gain new insights from looking at the history of real-world activity that spans a number of different departmentally focused IT applications and/or Workflow tools. There are a number of IT packages/tools that focus on this area, usually referred to as Business Activity Monitors (BAM). This is a growing area in the IT industry and is moving closer to real-time activity reporting.

- **Long-Running Transactions**—In the case of a business transaction that runs for a long time (in some cases many years—e.g., jail term of a convicted person), it may be useful to record the "status" information in an external and explicit way. This can help to "future-proof" the Events information.

---

are identified, there might be a lengthy implementation cycle. In these situations, it may be possible to implement differing levels of Event "granularity" (Event-capture points), depending on the degree of pre-knowledge and/ or the capability of a participating system (Human or IT). While this may not solve the whole problem, it often delivers a degree of early benefit through visibility of previously invisible behavior. This approach has the added benefit of learning-through-use—that is, the end users discover new ways of using the information, which might lead to a request to capture additional Events, and/or apply rules of association between one Event and another to provide new insights.

- **Local and Global Views**—This is the benefit associated with being able to create multiple "views" of Events in differing business contexts. It may be useful to present differing levels of Event detail or Event "Sets" to individuals and groups—in a global context, a country-level operation may be interested in local Events that have no meaning outside its borders and are therefore not useful to the global context. However, working on a standardized approach means that both global and local needs may be addressed in a flexible way that allows local Events to be made available to the global view, or the other way around. This can remove a significant barrier to adoption, by avoiding centralized definition/control, and by de-cluttering information based on any individual or groups' needs.

- **Re-purpose of Events**—Making Events explicit and external (and potentially, to subscribe to them based upon the needs of an individual or group) provides the opportunity to re-purpose them. That is, an Event originally captured for one purpose (within the context, for example, of an Operational Process) might be deemed useful elsewhere (such as in a Sales Process). This form of information re-use is often difficult (slow and costly) in a more traditional "Application-centric" architecture. If the Event is deemed to be widely publishable, the re-use of an Event can be as simple as an End-User creating a subscription to it (i.e., similar to subscribing to a Real Simple Syndication (RSS) newsfeed provided by, for example, the BBC).

- **Using Events as Proxies for Content**—Data Privacy and Protection concerns can create a significant barrier to implementation/adoption. One method of avoiding some of the knottier problems is to use an Event (e.g., Witness Statement Available) to act as a "proxy" for the Content (e.g., The Witness Statement). In some circumstances, it's fine to let trusted parties know that the Content exists over a reasonably open channel.

The power of thinking in terms of Events has lead to an increased focus on Event-driven architectures. In such architectures, Events are the primary units of architecture. When Events happen, messages are sent off, usually onto a message bus that many other computer programs are listening to. When a message is of interest to a program, that program reads the messages and does some work, and perhaps fires off more Events. In this way, Events become integration points between applications. The fact that Events lead to messages that are not linked to any specific receiver makes Event-driven architecture (EDA) very flexible, which some people refer to as "loosely-coupled." Loose coupling and externalized triggers are also foundational architectural principles of a Service-Oriented Architecture (SOA). In fact, an EDA and an SOA are two sides of the same coin, in the authors' opinion. While VPEC-T does not specify in any way the architecture of the solutions that will be constructed, IT departments that start thinking in terms of Events frequently build solutions that adhere to the principles of Event-driven architecture.

Fuzzy and Precise Event Information

Event information consists of both highly structured and precise, and highly unstructured and imprecise messages within a common Event "envelope" (general structure). For example, a movement-tracking system may receive highly structured signals from RFID or GPS devices, which are then converted into equally structured human-readable business Events. But the same system might also receive much more unstructured Event information, and possibly capture a "text" message on a mobile phone that might alert of a delay caused by heavy traffic. The emphasis is placed on the *value to the human consumer* as opposed to sometimes unhelpful, misplaced, information-engineering rigour. That's not to say, however, that over time loosely defined Event information won't benefit from being made more structured and precise. Likewise, some Event information needs to be semantic/syntax-precise from day one.

Information = Content—Not True!

- Think of Policies as rules (e.g., IF x THEN DO y). Rules are a type of information.

- Think of Content as the exchange of information (e.g., a paper Purchase Order or a discussion between workers or a Project Plan). Content is a type of information.

- Think of Events as the things that actually happen. Events can be described—the words and codes that describe the Event (e.g., Shipment 12345 Arrived Paris Hub at 10:00 12/01/2007) are a type of information.

- So "Information" within an Information System is made up of Policies, Events and Content.

Fuzzy Events—The Event information may not be as complete or as rigorous as, for example, a structured document or data record might require. However, it might be really useful to know that an Event has taken place, even if the information conveyed requires a degree of human interpretation. Maintaining separation between the Event and related Content makes it possible to get value from the Event information without confusing it with the necessarily precise business-Content information. This is because the Event and the Content have fundamentally different business purposes (as illustrated above). Recognizing this difference can be the key to avoiding lengthy data-modeling and data-standards work (around

Identity schemes and other codified data) and thus ensures a degree of business value is delivered as early as possible. The Event may not be interpretable by an IT system—but it may be of use to a person, in the same way a scribbled jotting on a sticky paper note might provide valuable information.

Precise Events—Paradoxically, the opposite is also true. Content, in the form of a conversation or audio/visual media, might be difficult for an IT system to consume and interpret, but is fine for human consumption. In this case, the separation can have the opposite benefit—the Event is always "IT-friendly," in the sense it can always be processed in the general sense of routing and subscription, and the Event "context information" may also be processed by rules and derive a new fact or implication.

The mobile phone—An Events Processor:

If I miss a call from you and I don't have your name in my phonebook (my "data model"), the phone still captures your number, and I can call you back or use another information resource (for example, my Outlook contacts) to determine who called. If you withhold your number, the Event may still be useful to me if I was expecting a call from you (i.e., Events are context-sensitive). Further, I can quickly see who I've received calls from by looking at my "calls received" Event list. I don't need to listen to hours of messages stored on my voicemail to hear the many (perhaps garbled!) voices and determine who called me and when they called.

Interestingly, our mobile phones can provide us with useful Event information, but many corporate IT applications can't. This is because either they lack a clear distinction between Content and Event and/or throw away Event information once they've used it internally. An example of this is: an application sets a Yes/No (Y/N) flag in a database when a shipment has arrived (ShipArriveFlag =Y). The application then "selfishly" uses this useful (albeit basic) Event information to trigger an internal action. The concept of the business

Event is lost (information expires) once the flag has been set, and is therefore unavailable for future processing. It's also often unclear whether the application in question is recording the *actual* arrival, or if the arrival "Event" is actually a by-product of paperwork being received. The Event (shipment physically received) and the Content (shipment paperwork) become indistinguishable in the IT application.

What's worse, if the IT application doesn't recognize a data item (e.g., the phone number of the person calling) it probably can't process it and, most likely, won't store it. As a consequence, a lot of business-useful information is lost, because we can only be informed of the Events that can be precisely predicted and represented in a data model.

Businesses and people work with real-world Events and content. IT can work very well with these concepts, too, when they are considered as discrete-but-related information objects which are not "owned" by a specific application. This distinction can also help us make better use of information that the Information Technology does not completely understand, by "red-flagging" it and passing it on to a human "interpreter."

Key questions to ask about Events:

- What are the key real-world Events that trigger a task or activity? E.g., Shipment Arrived, Aircraft Departed, Person Arrested, Person Crossed International Border, etc.
- What Events are expected and require action if they don't happen?
- Are there Events that you know about that would be of interest to others?
- Are the Events identifiable—can you associate the Event with a person or object, a location and a moment in time?
- What Events are useful to know about for the end user—how do they help achieve the outcome needed?

Trust Relationships

Understanding the effect of Trust-based relationships in business

To complete a VPEC-T analysis, Trust, the "softest," yet possibly most important dimension must be explored. Trust is easily the most difficult-to-define dimension and generally, the problem child of VPEC-T. This is because of a) the breadth of Trust as a topic in the context of real-world and human experience, and b) the vicious cycle of mistrust can be so damaging and hard to reverse.

Trust is an intriguing concept and can be expressed in many ways: Do I trust this person to keep a secret? Do I trust the government to keep information about me? Can I trust the information I discover on the Web? Do I trust a supplier to deliver per the terms of the agreed contract? What makes us trust one individual or organization over another? Most of us have a Trust relationship with the bank that looks

	Intimacy:
	• I know who I'm dealing with—they're familiar to me.
	• We talk about things that matter to me.
	• They understand me and relate to my situation.
	+ Credibility:
	• They've done this before—the service or product is proven to work.
Trust =	• I can ask others about their experience.
	• I have a sense that I'm dealing with experts—I get good ideas from the relationship.
	Over Risk:
	• Can I experiment without "betting the farm?"
	• What happens if I'm let down?
	• Could I get the same service cheaper?

after our cash that could be considered as blind-faith! Yet, we might be very suspicious of an independent financial advisor.

Trust is often the most discussed and debated topic when doing a VPEC-T analysis. From an IS/IT perspective, Trust is expressed in many ways: person-to-person relationships, system-to-person relationships, information pedigree, trust rating, the trust between business and IT provision—the list goes on.

Many of the "Trust relationships" of an organization are clearly understood by the organization. These relationships are often seen as critical to the business. These are the Trust relationships with employees, trading partners and end-customers. However, in this age of "information everywhere," the Trust relationships between all information consumers and providers need to be given greater visibility and measured. There are a number of examples where this is currently done. Third-party information services, such as credit-rating services, a system analogous to the eBay star rating, or a service-level agreement (SLA), all deal with some aspect of Trust rating. On top of this, a focus on Content pedigree (i.e., how do I know this information is correct?) fueled by regulatory control (such as Sarbanes-Oxley) and the Trust ratings of the consumer in Web-enabled, partially- or fully-virtualized businesses, are increasingly relevant.

Like the other dimensions, these aspects of Trust are important to explore early as they will likely impact:

- The adoption of an IT-enabled change—employees who don't trust don't adopt.
- The degree to which the IT solution supports employee-led innovation—"if I'm trusted to innovate, make sure the IT systems will allow it."
- The degree to which the IT solution supports regulatory mandates—"how can I be sure my company is complying with regulatory mandates if I don't know the pedigree of information that we have externally sourced?"

- The implications to existing and/or new user-authentication and access Policies—"I need to establish an employee's trust profile within my company."
- The degree to which the IT solution captures and reports the change of Trust ratings over time—"do my IT systems help me manage Trust?"

The amount of Trust associated with a business process or series of activities varies; this is influenced by many and diverse "soft" factors such as: experience, relationship maturity, relative value of the service, and competency.

Do Trust aspects impact?

The adoption of an IT-enabled change

The degree to which the IT solution supports employee-led innovation

The degree to which the IT solution supports regulatory mandates

The implications to existing and/or new user authentication and access policies

The degree to which the IT solution captures and reports the change of Trust ratings over time

We think it's interesting that we spend so much effort on *how systems trust users*. Perhaps we should spend equal effort on how *users trust information systems*.

Figure 3-3: The Impact of the Trust Dimension

Perhaps not surprisingly, one of the most frequently discussed aspects of Trust in VPEC-T analysis is the Trust relationship between the business and the IT function!

The Trust Experience

It's also interesting to consider that the degree of Trust between parties changes over time, and the declaration and sharing of the Values of the individuals or interacting business parties might change, depending on the degree of Trust. We're more willing to share our more intimate Values with a partner we trust. The same is true in a business relationship.

Why is Trust important to IS/IT projects? A Trust issue might be the single largest barrier to adoption of an IT solution that is intended to deliver an important business outcome. Having an awareness of Trust as a broad topic, and more specifically, the Trust relationships in play during both the execution of the project and the operation of the solution, simply reduces risk.

From the perspective of the User of an IT solution, it might be appropriate to consider the Trust Relationship aspects of information being exchanged between parties. It may affect the roll-out timeline and the scope of functionality at each stage of an IT solution implementation—as a greater degree of Trust may need to be established between different Users (e.g., Police and Prosecution Agents), and between the Users and the IT provider, before the final outcome can be realized. It may be necessary to demonstrate Commitment and Capability before the IT solution is fully adopted.

Understanding the degree of Trust at each point along a process and how it changes over time is critical to the adoption of new or modified interactions, and the ultimate successful delivery of the desired outcome. Trust is the basis of business and human interaction. However, it's normally not considered in business requirements specification (with the possible exception of a very narrow and slightly perverse exploration into the IT solution's trust of the user!).

Given its importance, should we not think about Trust right upfront? We believe thinking about this dimension will reveal important money-saving and/or risk-reducing insights, when considered in conjunction with the Values, Policies, Events and Content.

Key questions to ask about Trust:

- What are they key Trust relationships at work in this information system?
- Is there a risk of damaging a Trust relationship when implementing change?
- Is there an opportunity to develop the Trust relationships?
- What is the Trust relationship between the users and the IT providers?
- What will be the impact of Trust issues to the adoption of the IT solution?
- Specific focus areas:
  - How do we know the information received is correct— What is its pedigree?
  - Can we implement a community trust rating system (e.g., like an eBay star-rating)—How do we measure Trust, and do we care?
  - For organizations and employees—How much freedom to act is allowed—How trusted are the employees and how is that manifested?
  - For organizations and their consumers—What is the Trust relationship? How important is it? Can the information system support it?
  - For information service consumers—Can I trust 3rd-party information providers?
  - For the constituents of a federated IT system—Can we implement Trust-based user authentication and access?

Putting Your Understanding To Work

A more thorough understanding of VPEC-T generally leads to propagation of the technique. Nothing succeeds like success, and once VPEC-T has a few successes, people tend to be curious.

Many practitioners do not at first explain that they are using VPEC-T—they just do it! They introduce the dimensions into their work and let the improved analysis have a positive effect. Just thinking in terms of an information system, rather than focusing on the IT solutions, has benefit. Using the rest of the VPEC-T thinking framework amplifies the effect.

Eventually, the third or fourth time someone hears you talk about Values or Trust or describe the Events and Content in terms of Events and Content, they will start to ask why you are using these terms or thinking this way. The next chapter will help you experiment with VPEC-T and provide some more practical examples of how it's used.

Chapter 4

VPEC-T Analysis Applied: The Art of Clarity

When putting VPEC-T to work, it is important to keep in mind that it is a thinking framework, not a formal methodology. To the authors, a thinking framework is a way of asking questions in a structured manner to reveal important information. So, with VPEC-T, there isn't a step-by-step process to the analysis. Instead, there are just the five words to consider, each of which represents a different dimension of an information system. By asking questions about these words you provoke thinking in yourself and others. VPEC-T analysis is designed to be *complementary* to your field of expertise and experience, and the frameworks and methods you already use.

In a nutshell, we've found that as people use VPEC-T they develop their own approaches to applying it—which vary by their own fields of expertise.

You may end up developing your own list of questions associated with each word. You may come up with a document template for the analysis. The technique used to capture the output of the analysis isn't particularly important. It can be tailored to suit a particular situation. It is important, however, to capture information under each VPEC-T dimension. The emphasis might vary—but all should be considered. The starting point for analysis varies depending on the business problem being addressed. In certain situations, it may be most appropriate to start by examining the highest level Values Systems that affect business behavior without regard to any specific, detailed processes. Understanding the Values in play may help organize the analysis of the Policies, Events, Content, and Trust issues. In other situations, it might be more useful to start with the important business Events and Content, mapped in terms of the business processes or themes. In yet other situations, it may be most relevant to start with a focus on Policies, if, for example, regulatory control is the current burning business issue.

VPEC-T as a form of Storytelling

Once you start using VPEC-T, you quickly find that it is a powerful way of boiling down the important elements of what makes an organization work. The representation of the information in each dimension is far more like a story than any other traditional form of IT documentation.

Many of the elements of VPEC-T are story-like. They describe what people think, what they believe, how they act, whether they trust each other. Even when the focus is on highly tangible elements like real-world events and the content of business documents, the context is still on how people interact with those elements as they do their work.

For this reason, people tend to remember the results of VPEC-T analysis. Stories are memorable. The search for conflicts in Values and Policies is like a mystery. The way that Trust is created or destroyed is a study in psychology. Events and Content are pieces of a puzzle that are being fit into a larger structure. It is possible that information systems analysis may be accurately summarized as a form of information-systems storytelling.

This flexibility ensures that the focus of the dialogue is aligned with the current business challenges from the outset. It is important, however, to fold in all five dimensions—with the appropriate emphasis—to expose possible contradictions, tensions, and surface useful insights.

Defining the Guiding Rules for Business Transformation

VPEC-T thinking is useful when defining the guiding rules—the *principles*—for business transformation. There are many professional communities involved in defining these principles, and then using them to design "blueprints" for new business processes enabled by IT. At an enterprise level, such blueprints are often known as the "Enterprise Architecture."

Many business and IT strategists and architects understand the importance of such principles and have been taking a principle-led approach for some time. We will discuss what's different with VPEC-T

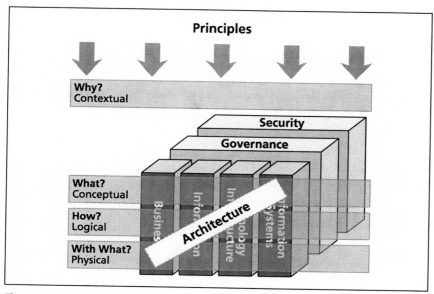

Figure 4-1: VPEC-T—Related Principles

later in this section (see also the Chapter 6 interviews); for now, the simple answer is it ensures that architectures are aligned and balanced, and that the particulars of business-process engineering or IT engineering do not dominate in the initial analysis.

Using the dimensions of Values, Policies, Events, Content, and Trust to guide the thinking and test the emerging principles (applied in a similar way to SWOT analysis) helps ensure that outcome-affecting aspects are covered.

Strengths	Weakness
Opportunities	Threats

Table 4-1: SWOT Analysis Grid

Perhaps most importantly, conflicts between differing Values and Polices, or between organizations and their Trust relationships, surface as a consequence. Using VPEC-T prevents important facets such as possibilities, issues, needs, concerns, and tensions from being ignored. Examples of these facets are given at the end of this section (see also the Chapter 6 interviews).

Values	Policies	Trust
Events	Content	

Table 4-2: VPEC-T Analysis Grid

It might be useful to visualize the process. Imagine a workshop initiated to derive such principles. The facilitator writes up the VPEC-T dimensions on the whiteboard and suggests that the group keep these in focus while discussing potential principles. Next, she writes up four headings on separate flip charts:

- Business Principles—the business drivers that define the need for change or business rules constraining the change program.

- Governance Principles—the guiding rules about who will make what decision in delivering the desired change.
- Solution Principles—statements that constrain the solution design and implementation.
- Tension Points—points that create risk to successful implementations due to, for example, differing values or conflicting policies—they may be irresolvable, but must be recognized and managed.

It's worth noting here that it isn't necessary to organize the principles under the VPEC-T dimensions—just use them as a guide for arriving at a principle.

Our imaginary facilitator then explains that the group should think about principles in the three categories and make a note of any tension points that arise. The facilitator suggests that the group look at tension points at the end of the session, and for each point, decide on an action to:

- negotiate and resolve,
- accept and tolerate,
- innovate to resolve,
- escalate to a higher authority.

The value of this VPEC-T structured and facilitated discussion is in the collective understanding of the derived principles and agreed approach to tension-point resolution. The information gathered provides a stronger foundation for further work, such as the development of an IT Strategy, Enterprise Architecture, or the outcome-affecting considerations for a business transformation program.

Here are some examples of the insights gained from a VPEC-T analysis that inform the creation of principles:

- The impact to IT of differences in the Value Systems which affect business operations across geographies.

- The value of common Business Event visibility.
- The need for stronger business/IT policy governance.
- The recognition of the need to improve Trust Relationships to remove adoption barriers.
- The need for a focus on Content standards and Policies for *specific* information exchanges and identification schemes (such as People, Objects, Locations, and Events).

In this section we've discussed how VPEC-T can be used in the context of a facilitated session of, for example, department heads and other subject matter experts. VPEC-T can go further and deeper. In the next section, we explore how VPEC-T can be applied during a more detailed analysis of business processes, activities, and interactions.

Analyzing End-to-End Processes

To help give context to a VPEC-T analysis of business activities, Business Analysts and IS Architects might find it is useful to imagine for a moment that the familiar models to describe a business didn't exist. Imagine a business without an Organization Chart, a set of Process Diagrams, or Financial Models. How might we think about describing the business in a way that represents its highly inter-connected, unstructured, and structured operations?

Think of "processes," not in a static and mechanical sense, but as a series of more abstract themes (or threads) of interaction that run in all directions across the enterprise. On each thread, imagine a series of beads. These beads represent a business capability or service, (a contracted capability) either of which is triggered by real-world events. Each bead undertakes specific tasks and creates interim or final outcomes.

Using this concept helps focus on specific strands of behavior and provides context to a discussion about the VPEC-T dimensions, without becoming constrained by more rigorous process-based methods. This is a neutral and flexible way of describing business

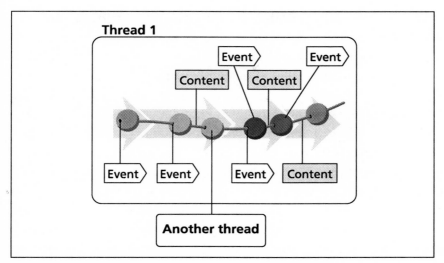

Figure 4-2: An Example of a Threads and Beads Diagram

processes or value chains, with the primary purpose of discussing the VPEC-T dimensions rather than, for example, the engineering of formal process steps.

However, it's possible to use almost any technique that helps provide the context for the overall interaction between tasks, activities, competencies, components, and services. For example, VPEC-T dimensions might be added to formal process analysis techniques, such as Value Chain Analysis, Swim-Lane Modeling, or Interaction Design. What's important is to make sure that the VPEC-T dimensions are discussed and any insights recorded.

> *The graphical representation of threads and beads is similar to other process, workflow, or value-chain analysis diagrams; however, the de-emphasis on the expression of formal process, and emphasis on the core VPEC-T dimensions are critical differences. To put it another way, it's the discussion behind the diagram that is important. The purpose of the threads and beads diagram is nothing more than to provide context for the VPEC-T discussion.*

Getting back to the threads and beads approach, threads can be used to represent a business theme or an end-to-end process. To help with the distinction between process and theme, it's useful to think of the process as being owned by someone, whereas a theme isn't. However, both processes and themes are focused on delivering one or more business outcomes. For example, within the context of a government's drive to improve its Criminal Justice services to a citizen, a thread might be the theme of "Victim and Witness Support" and the outcomes might be "Improved Witness Protection" and "Post-Trial Victim Follow-up." The thread might describe an existing or future process, or combination of processes, and themes.

So, in summary, threads and beads describe how a business outcome will be achieved. They provide a simple way to capture current interactions and a structure for brainstorming future ways of working. In either case, they maintain a focus on the desired business outcomes. The business outcomes provide the basis of the VPEC-T discussion along each thread and at each bead within it. Often, the most illuminating insights will be gained by examining multiple threads of interaction and comparing the VPEC-T dimensions of one thread to another across different business objectives (desired outcomes).

Shared Service Discovery

Many businesses focus on removing duplication and improving agility, which is leading them to initiate efforts to discover candidates for shared services (both human-based and/or technology-based). Understanding the nature of the cross-overs and joins between threads of interaction is at the heart of the discovery and implementation of shared services.

The Systems-thinking basis of VPEC-T Analysis lends itself to Service Orientation and component engineering. However, it is designed to communicate to the broadest possible audience across both the business and IT worlds. It structures discussion in such a way that specifications of services and the associate triggering events, contracts (or Policies), information exchanges (Events and Content), and Trust rating are made explicit.

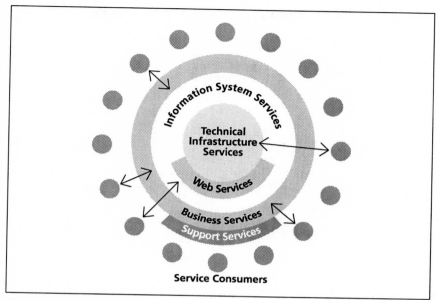

Fig: 4-3: Shared Services

Taking the Lid Off the "Magic Happens Here Box"

Perhaps one of the most compelling illustrations of the difference between the VPEC-T approach and traditional process analysis represented in a process-flow diagram is the "Magic Happens Here Box."

The "flat" nature of a process model can create the illusion that "All Boxes are Equal." A box that describes a highly automated and industrialized activity might sit alongside a much less-defined process step—one that is essentially a collection of loosely defined behaviors that might be supported by the extensive use of user-selected IT (see later section on Shadow IT).

The "language" of the process model lacks the richness to describe such behavior in a way that is consistent with the automated steps, and as a result, is often poorly described—"Magic Happens Here." In contrast, because the VPEC-T approach places emphasis on the dimensions of Values, Policies, Events, Content, and Trust, it is possible to consistently describe both industrialized activities and the more people-oriented behaviors.

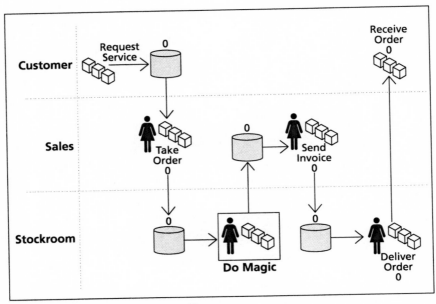

Figure 4-4: The Magic Happens Here

The requirements for both transaction and interaction-type behaviors can be articulated under the same VPEC-T headings.

However, regardless of the particular business need or the number of threads involved, the challenge is in recognizing and then meeting the needs of each stakeholder group, and creating a unified system of values (Value System). This may require several discussions and workshops to reach agreement.

Finally, the simplified nature of the threads and beads approach provides a common mechanism for describing the interactions without being hampered by a focus on:

- the existence or absence of a recognized process,
- the degree to which the behavior is automated or otherwise "industrialized,"
- organizational domains and geographical boundaries,
- the perceived achievability of a desired outcome based on a narrow view of current practice.

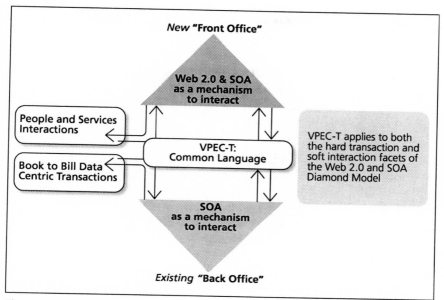

Figure 4-5: The Diamond Model

Where's the Beef?

Given that VPEC-T is a way of thinking rather than a methodology, we won't attempt to define exactly what a VPEC-T-influenced deliverable would look like. The results of the VPEC-T analysis will become embedded in deliverables your project will produce. The findings of the analysis might be included in, for example, a business or IT strategy report, they might be documented as a set of principles for an Enterprise Architecture, or they might be documented as input to a business transformation program design.

VPEC-T dimensions might also, for example, be captured in Service Specifications in a situation where a formal definition of Services is needed. Examples include: defining a Service-Oriented Architecture (SOA), understanding the services from a Software as a Service (SaaS) delivered by an enterprise business software provider, or when documenting the third-party business services within a Supply Chain.

However, the most important outcome is the common understanding between the business stakeholders, the business operators,

VPEC-T and Wikis

Most of the time VPEC-T analysis uncovers insights that apply to many of the information systems at a company. Values and Policies rarely apply to only one information system. Events and Content can trigger actions or act as a conduit between information systems. For this reason, it is useful to have a shared repository for the results of analysis and research created using VPEC-T. The discussion of Values related to one information system can be the starting point, when those Values are revisited in the context of another information system. The same is true for all the other VPEC-T dimensions.

Wikis are well-suited to this purpose. Wiki pages can be easily edited so that a large group can add their thoughts and insights to a group of pages. The pages can be organized and reorganized quite quickly. Wikis can capture knowledge that would otherwise have no home. In effect, wikis are a form of content that captures the often unstructured information that VPEC-T creates.

and the IT providers. A common understanding that is expressed in the simple, real-world-aligned language of Values, Policies, Events, Content and Trust, and is focused on delivering better IT!

Golden Principles for Testing VPEC-T Analysis

VPEC-T can be applied at varying levels and stages within a project. People using VPEC-T have found the following points useful in undertaking VPEC-T analysis:

- Is business language being used? Are the desired business outcomes clear?
- Are unnecessary process detail and implementation aspects being avoided?

- Would a potential consumer be willing to explore the system using the service described? Do they have enough information?
- Could the findings be presented to a business sponsor or governance body?
- Could an Action Plan be created? Can we identify opportunities/options and make clear recommendations?
- Have areas of risk to the planned IT-enabled change been identified?
- Would the output be useful to an IT Architect?
- Can the output be applied to automated and non-automated situations?
- Have the VPEC-T dimensions been captured and tested— by confirming their validity with subject matter experts and/or walk-through sessions?

Of course, the quality of the analysis can only be assessed by the stakeholders and subject matter experts. The important point is that we are all using the same language which lessens the risk of misunderstanding or otherwise obscuring facts (deliberate or not!).

A Process That Evolves

Similarly, there are no particular rights or wrongs for the way the VPEC-T analysis is executed. However, here are some guiding considerations:

- Be prepared to run several VPEC-T workshops for each focus area and allow for significant refinement and even dramatic changes in "facts" from one workshop to the next.
- Don't expect to cover all five core dimensions in one go. It's likely that only one or two will be covered in a session.
- The dimensions of Values and Trust might be hard to uncover and developing Trust over time will be required
- Be prepared to take sensitive issues to the Executive Sponsor.

- Be prepared for contradictions and tensions between various Policies and differing Values. The goal is for such conflict to surface early.
- Be aware of differing levels of VPEC-T scope: market, ecosystem, company, department, individual.
- Ensure that descriptive language is simple, relevant, and unambiguous.

General Applicability

Practitioners are applying VPEC-T in an increasing number of business situations (see also Practitioner Interviews). In general, organizations might find the VPEC-T approach useful when planning and executing change projects that include one or more of the following:

- Planning and executing business transformation programs
- Reducing business complexity
- Embracing new business models in the connected world
- Highly Federated business situations (e.g. global supply chains, governments)
- Balancing Central Control with Local Freedom-To-Act
- Reducing IT Time-to-Market barriers
- Developing Shared Services and IT Commoditization (e.g. Software-as-a-Service, such as that offered by Salesforce.com) strategies
- Developing a business system model to take advantage of Service-Oriented Architecture and Web 2.0 technologies
- Developing Semantic-Web ("Web 3.0") strategies and new information models that combine tacit and explicit information
- Developing Event-based technology strategies (e.g. RFID and BAM)
- Developing Managed Service Provision business models (e.g. Supply Chain intermediaries or SaaS Providers)
- Developing "Change-ready" IT strategies

- Developing post-M&A IS/IT strategies
- Developing customizable services to clients without perpetuating "point solutions"
- Dealing with complex interacting Systems of Value (e.g. Governments)
- Dealing with complex information-privacy and protection concerns

VPEC-T is a practical thinking framework for Information Systems analysis—a way of thinking that is straightforward but works in complex situations. VPEC-T is generally useful and can be adopted by all: business leaders, IT leaders, change agents, and business and IT practitioners. It can be applied in numerous ways. However, the aim is always the same—a common understanding that is expressed in the straightforward, real-world-aligned language of Values, Policies, Events, Content and Trust, and is focused on delivering better IT for business and people.

Understanding VPEC-T is something that happens in stages. Once you start using VPEC-T, your understanding of how it works increases and the way that it changes your thinking expands. You become used to thinking about the Values in play in a situation or the Policies that are causing a conflict. Applying VPEC-T is a journey.

Chapter 5

Externalization & Adoption Engineering: Tackling the Biggest Picture

One startling aspect of the Web is just how much information sharing is taking place. It's startling how new ways of working emerge when information and services, from many different sources, are available to anyone, anytime, anywhere. These new ways of working aren't the preserve of the corporate strategists—communities of people, both as employees and as individuals, are generating them. In fact, the IT we use as an individual is often more sophisticated than the IT we use at work.

The world is exponentially more connected with each connection, which in turn fuels more connections. This level of (increasing) connectedness is unprecedented. At the same time, we are witnessing an unprecedented level of "business-technology fusion." People and machines, business and IT, are becoming fundamentally fused. Technology literacy is at an unprecedented level. Yet despite this fusion, the "business/IT divide" is getting worse, not better. Business outcomes sought from IT-enabled business transformation are as elusive as ever.

How might we think about this unprecedented world of *connectedness* and *business-technology fusion*, and how might we act to bring about business transformation in this context?

We believe that it's useful to understand the trend from an Information Systems perspective—which then leads to an understanding of a new style of response. We call the trend "Externalization" and the response "Adoption Engineering."

"Externalization"—The Information Systems Trend

Information Technology has been evolving to help people get data out of the database and share it. The Web model supports and reinforces the move towards connectedness. And at the same time, standards have been adopted which are leading to commoditization and ubiquitous connectivity of IT. And so it's no surprise that people have become more IT-literate and are using this new literacy to make more connections and share more information with ever more people. This connectedness is regenerating itself further and further onward.

The business trend of globalization is well understood—perhaps though, this has more to do with the ever-expanding web of connections than we imagined. The IT trend of the Web model is also well understood. The problem is that the two trends are seen as just that—*two* trends: a business trend and an IT trend. Debates still rage about which leads, and which follows. Many agree the two are themselves, of course, highly connected—but this is still expressed as a business and an IT view. There is another way to view the two trends—as a unified Information System, where behavior, people, and technology are playing parts.

We call this Information Systems trend *"Externalization,"* and the response to the trend *"Adoption Engineering."*

The Externalization trend is moving toward a world where *any* information is usable by *any* person or *any* machine. Where the identity of people, things, business Events, and machines are uniquely and ubiquitously known, not just internally to a given business, but just like a Web site's www address is known to anyone. Where the "applications" a business finds useful are available securely over the Web to all customers, employees, and suppliers. Such services are ubiquitously available and mass customizable. In this Externalized world, IT labor requirements are vastly reduced, as businesses use "shared services" over the Web, as opposed to each business implementing

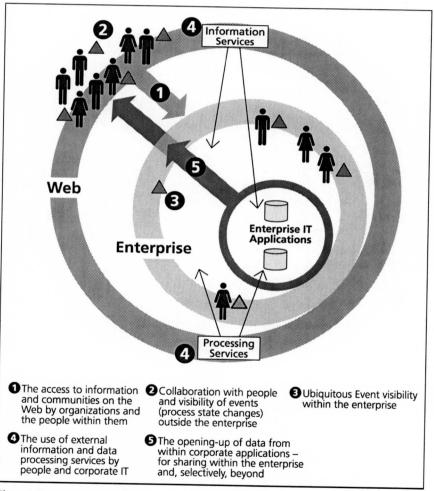

❶ The access to information and communities on the Web by organizations and the people within them

❷ Collaboration with people and visibility of events (process state changes) outside the enterprise

❸ Ubiquitous Event visibility within the enterprise

❹ The use of external information and data processing services by people and corporate IT

❺ The opening-up of data from within corporate applications – for sharing within the enterprise and, selectively, beyond

Figure 5-1: Externalization

and managing its own IT. And value isn't inherent within a software product—it's now just part of the easy-to-consume service (contrast an IT product which needs to be implemented and managed by each business, versus a service operationally available to any business over the Web). In this world, market forces, consumer power, and employee power dominate in the evolution of these services.

Many of us have heard of Software as a Service, SOA, Blogs, and Mashups, but many in the technology community are also considering the rapidly emerging standards, trends, and services that will fuel the move toward even more externalized information and services (See Figure 5-2).

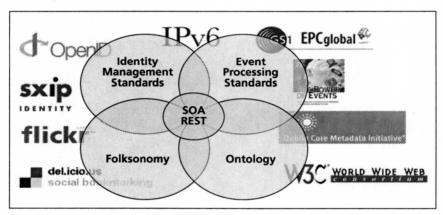

Figure 5-2: Web2.0/3.0—Not Business as Usual

So, it is no longer a case of "Business as Usual." There are new challenges that cannot be addressed by doing the same thing better. Instead, there is a need for "innovation," to "Change the Game" around two primary themes:

1. Companies need to do business in markets that are increasingly open and therefore more competitive. Globalization and connectedness have introduced new competitors, new markets, and new business models, all of which offer new opportunities and threats.

2. People have changed their relationship with Technology. It is now an accepted part of many people's ordinary lives, and it is people as consumers that have driven the new generation of Web 2.0 technologies. They now expect to use these same capabilities in their workplace.

Technology has driven these two changes, but it's misleading to think of this as "Information Technology"—a.k.a., old-school IT. Instead it is a new generation of people-centric technology based around the architecture of the Web, mixing Information and free-roaming communication technologies.

These themes have a common thread—the move from an "*internal*" view of the world to "***external***" views of the world.

From an IT perspective, the rise in the adoption of standards such as SOA, Web 2.0, and the semantic Web (Web 3.0) are all representative of a foundational, underlying trend. If real-time integrated business intelligence, composite applications, mashups, and Software as a Service are examples of the "how," ***Externalization*** is the expression of the "*what*"—the underlying IS trend, and more specifically, the agenda to exploit it. From a business perspective one can observe three business drivers that appear repeatedly across all industries:

- the development of new customer and client interactions,
- the evolution of the supply chain notably toward the "demand chain," and
- the adoption of new business models.

All three cross-industry drivers are heavily dependent on technology and all three are driven by the "external" view of the world.

So, what is Externalization? There is a fundamental difference between the way the Web works and traditional enterprise IT systems. The Web starts with the premise that any resource—such as business information or services—can be used by anyone for any purpose. Traditional enterprise IT systems start the other way round—with a *constrained, internal* perspective—usually in support of specific business processes. If internalization can be thought of as incorporating information and services for yourself (be it a person or organization), Externalization can be thought of as a condition where your information and services can be usable by any person or any machine.

In a practical sense, Externalization is the underlying IS trend toward **ubiquitous information sharing and access to services**—where information and services are available to anyone or any machine, for any purpose. Contrast a business application specifically designed to support a set of business processes with a mashup service specifically designed so that **anyone** can use it to support **their** specific goals. Consider Externalization as the IS trend of:

- Breaking apart the concepts of applications and databases to expose the business-meaningful parts of an Information System and, at the same time, making tacit, human knowledge and behavior explicit,
- Integrating externally owned information sources and services of value to the Business Information System,
- Consuming and publishing business-meaningful events within and outside the enterprise.

Externalization also invites management to consider whether there are existing services provided on the Web first, before they decide to implement services internally within the organization.

Shadow IT

A special form of Externalization taking place in many organizations today is "Shadow IT"—that is, the non-corporate "Information Technology" that people employ in their day-to-day work. Many processes or other threads of interaction work very well without top-down design—the office staff and shop-floor workers focus on getting the job done, *despite* centrally mandated processes, procedures and systems.

White Wire Strategy

Chris Anderson (of *The Long Tail*) talks about "the black wire and the white wire." The black wire connects Chris to the corporate network, which is connected to the Internet. The white wire is a standard consumer connection to the Internet.

The black wire constrains the information and services to which Chris has access. The white wire doesn't. It seems to be faster, too.

This is a thought provoking perspective, which ultimately leads to fascinating questions for organizations such as: "Why do I have the black wire? Why would I implement my own corporate IT services? Why wouldn't I take them from the Web?"

These are quite simple, yet deep questions. Consider corporately owned networks, PCs, applications, databases, and data centers. And then consider the point of all of these things—to support business outcomes!

Given business outcomes depend more than ever on the connectedness of an organization with the world via the Web. There is a logic to using services on the Web, because, by definition, these have global reach and their providers have often figured out, in an IT sense at least, how to secure information in the outside world. They are "white wires" by default. Staff, contractors, suppliers, customers—IT of other organizations—can all make use of the information and services.

Some of these questions are starting to be taken seriously. Real-world conversations on global IT strategy sometimes start with "why do we have corporate IT?" It is, of course, a provocative question, but that's the point—to start from this perspective and work back, rather than the other way round. Questions, such as "what helps serve our business outcomes more—more application functionality or more connectedness?" are also being asked.

There is clearly a business need for corporate IT, but explicitly exploring "White Wire Strategy" questions helps, in the least, test long-held assumptions, and, at best, can shine the light on new possibilities in the here and now.

Shadow IT—or How business Information Systems Actually Work

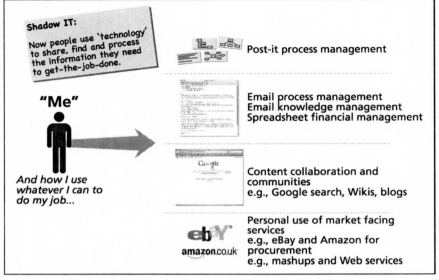

Figure 5-3: Shadow IT

While employee creativity can be seen as beneficial in many situations, the opportunities and risks presented by "Shadow IT" need to be assessed if we are to understand how the business actually processes information. It needs to be considered within the context of the overall business Information System, of which it is often a significant part. While there may be no appetite for draconian restrictions on the use of this personal use of IT, there is a real and present issue for corporate governance if "Shadow IT" remains invisible.

The reason for this urgency lies within the expanded personal access to information-based services that many of us have access to today. In the past, the IT systems available to me restricted my access to corporate mainframe or departmental systems. Over time, more and more information resources became available, first on the corporate PC networks, then on the Web and via ubiquitous mobile-device access. Today, it's often easier to get information from the Web than from our corporate systems (internal Knowledge Management systems are being substituted with Google/Wikipedia, for example). Not only that, but it is now possible to easily store, back up, and process data outside the four walls of the enterprise. This may or not present an issue for corporate data privacy and intellectual property. However, not knowing how the corporate Information System is using such external services is probably a high-risk strategy. At the very least, it would seem useful to know if there is a best practice to be harvested and/or to know more about the pedigree of external information that is being used to aid decision-making.

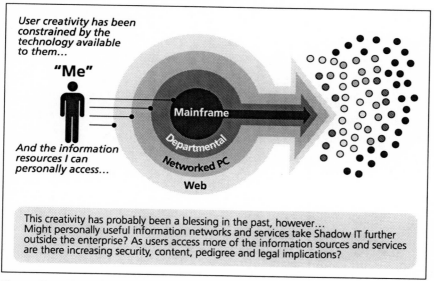

Figure 5-4: The Explosion of Available Information Resources

"Adoption Engineering"—The Information Systems Response

In the context of the Externalization trend, where connections between business and between people are growing exponentially, it is little wonder that many of the leading practices for "IT-enabled business change" are being found wanting. Such approaches were developed in the context of the solid four walls of the enterprise, out-of-the-box enterprise-scale software packages, and all the process predictability that goes with that.

To make matters worse, it seems the term "IT-enabled business change" immediately creates issues by language used:

- The business/IT separation is reinforced by use of both words independently—are you "*business*" **or** "*IT*"?
- *Change* implies a "to-be" state—a "one day, some day" mentality, rather than the new Business As Usual.
- And that someone will be doing the *change to* someone else rather than inviting them to adopt new behaviors and services, with the subtext: "You are broken and you therefore need fixing"—not a great vote-winner!

Considering *why* an IT or business *service* will be *adopted* from the outset, and *engineering* the adoption, seems the key to answering this question of why IT is useful sometimes, but less so other times. Perhaps it's worth going to the dictionary to make the point:

> *Adoption*: to take and follow (a course of action, for example) by choice or assent: *adopt a new technique or service.* To take up and make one's own: *adopt a new idea.*
> *Engineering*: to plan, manage, and make so, through skillful application of proven techniques.

So, bearing the above definitions in mind, *Adoption Engineering* is the label we use to describe the re-shaping of the way we think about IS and the use of IT in business that embraces constant change. It is also a response to the Externalization trend. VPEC-T is an *Information Systems thinking framework* for *Adoption Engineering*. Adoption Engineering is a family of approaches, frameworks, and styles which focus on:

- *How new behavior, enabled by IT solutions, will be **adopted** by the users and other stakeholders, and*
- *How to understand the desired business outcomes in such a way that a focus can be maintained on engineering them.*

Adoption Engineering comprises a broad family of techniques—some of them well known, others less so. VPEC-T is part of the DNA in this family as it underpins many of the techniques in a way that combines business and IT—or to be more precise, in an Information Systems way. VPEC-T is the common language of Adoption Engineering. This is why we felt it made sense to publish an introductory IS and VPEC-T book first—this one!

Other techniques in the Adoption Engineering family:

- Specific workshop techniques for solving complex problems
- Business-IT visualization
- How to get the most from/survive in an Externalized world
- Externalization Agenda—stop fussing, adopt and consume!
- Technology Leadership styles
- How to make sense of technology trends
- New Enterprise Architecture approaches and SOA thinking
- CxO communication—Outcomes and Adoption are all that matter
- From Business Transformation to Business Adoption—a new Business-As-Usual
- Managing Complexity by understanding what matters and what is being adopted
- Responding to changing markets and commoditization

These are shown to provide a flavor for the topic and are not discussed further in this book.

Pull versus Push

It's fascinating that, to the common observer, an aircraft appears to be pushed upwards by the air beneath its wings. In reality, it is the vacuum created above the wings that pulls the aircraft into the sky. Wings that work create a pull, not a push. And perhaps it is so with transformation. To the common observer, there is a to-be goal and specific changes are sought to push people toward the goal. This is interesting, as no one likes being told they are broken and that they need fixing! In reality, it is perhaps more through a focus on adoption—"why would I adopt this?" rather than change—"you need to change!" which creates the pull for the organization and its people to behave in new ways, and the pull to evolve structures and systems toward the goal. *Carl Bate*

We hope that you find VPEC-T interesting and that you will try it for yourself.

Two additional sections have been added to provide more information and to allow the reader to harvest the experience of others. The next chapter in the book is a composite interview that shows how others who have used the thinking framework think about VPEC-T and have used it successfully.

We also hope that you may want to share experiences with others who are putting VPEC-T to work. We invite you to join the conversation at *www.LIThandbook.com.*

Chapter 6

Interviews: The Value of VPEC-T in the Real World

To help bring VPEC-T to life, we have interviewed a number of people who are using VPEC-T.

Below are excerpts from 12 of the interviews. We've broken the results into segments that particularly highlight each of the five dimensions, and one segment that highlights all five dimensions working together.

Some characteristics of the companies have been altered to respect the Trust relationships we have with our sources, but all of these examples are real-world case studies and are taken from actual interview transcripts.

Some of the interviews are with executives offering leadership in the business/IT divide.

Others are senior IT-enabled business change practitioners, such as Business Analysts and Enterprise Architects.

While the focus is on VPEC-T, it's important to remember that all of the interviewees are using VPEC-T to complement, rather than replace the frameworks they already use.

Interviewer: Dan Woods (DW)
Interviewees: A Practitioner (AP)

Values

Interview #1: *The task of creating a new enterprise architecture and business/IT blueprint for a global busi-
ness revealed conflicting Value Systems, and a
resulting misaligned incentive system, among the
stakeholders.*

DW: You were sent in to create a new "business and
IT blueprint" for a company-wide transformation
program, and to create an "enterprise architecture"
group that would support the business and IT in
delivering the blueprint. How did you begin?

AP: We looked at two different aspects of how a framework might help us guide the thinking around the
delivery of some of those key elements, in terms of
delivering an enterprise structure within this global
company.

The first example is actually around a whole governance piece. Typically, within the organization,
you find conflicting Value Systems, and we actually
took this as a *Value-System* view, around how the
company and the delivery of the company's IT is
actually governed.

This company had a very classic example of an
operational organization that was responsible for the
day-to-day running of the company's infrastructure.
And they had an organization that was responsible
for the delivery of change within that company's
infrastructure, which covered new development and
that type of thing. There was no clear governance
process established between the two.

The goal was to create a governance structure that said, "This is how you resolve the *Value Systems* that exist, and the conflicts that those Value Systems generate between the operational and change aspects of the software development lifecycle."

That was very useful in terms of actually starting off with a picture of what "run the company" and "change the company" looked like, where they overlapped, and where the *Value Systems* between those two created tension, which gave us the framework to set up the governance process you put in place to resolve those tensions.

This was done purely in an IT/IS bubble. It had nothing to do with the business.

The next thing that we learned was that there was a *Value System* that the company needed to have, which nobody owned, and that Value System was needed to dictate how aspects of the company could be integrated at an enterprise level. It was almost like a set of group functions that would allow you to pull together the major elements of the company. Divisions like risk and compliance fit into that. A single view of customers fits into that.

So what we said was, "actually, at the moment, we're organized around two key functions: 'run the company' and 'change the company.'" Nobody owned "integrate the company."

And, in fact, the Value System associated with "integrate the company" didn't fit with the level at which we were then pitching the IT architecture.

So we actually turned it around the other way. We looked at the Value System and said, "Who, fundamentally, is the actor for this? Oh, actually, it's the CEO."

So when you start to think about integrating the company's functions, the business owner who actually owns that *Value System* is the CEO, in addition to the board of the company.

DW: Does this tell us there's a sort of dysfunction in the organizational structure?

AP: It means there's a whole set of questions that the business has given IT about cost-income ratio reduction that they were never going to get to, because, in fact, the Value System associated with that was not recognized as being owned by anybody.

DW: So, in fact, the *Value System* probably wasn't understood as a discrete thing. So, it was kind of like the 800-pound gorilla no one could see?

AP: We think it's a very good example of taking the VPEC-T framework, and using it to help recognize the absence of things, or the absence of *owners* of things, that should be articulated as elements within the company's governance model.

DW: This seems to be one of those cases where VPEC-T was able to expose an issue in corporate governance, when you thought you were just setting out to solve an IT problem.

AP: Absolutely. You can't drive through that type of IT program unless the corporate governance is in place to manage it. One of the phenomena that we discovered was that the company's incentive program was misaligned with IT goals. The business-unit heads are typically incentivized on a yearly basis. Most specific IT programs are not one-year programs.

So when you are looking at how you integrate a company, and you get consistent models of data that you've then got to customize, the timescale for doing that is typically outside of the *Value Systems* for those business-unit heads, because their bonus process is a on a yearly cycle.

So, in its most basic form, it can create a situation where the business community mistrusts everything the IT group is doing because it may affect their bonus. It's a *Trust* issue in its absolute simplest form.

DW: Did this problem arise because of a lack of recognition of *information systems,* as opposed to *information technology?*

AP: No. I think, for me, it's fundamentally around the fact that, if you're going to land a long-term strategic IT answer, you have to land it at the right level of the organization, and that typically isn't people that the organization has incentivized on a yearly basis.

DW: Why was the company looking for an "enterprise architecture," and why were they then looking to build a group to support it?

AP: Because the *Value System* of a company doesn't recognize the need at some level.

They'd gone through that tactical exercise of, "Here's a package, put it in," or, "just make this change here." Systems built on that paradigm are built to a point where they're essentially barren. We couldn't do anything else with them. We hit a wall. It's "architecture death." You're continually taking out of the pool without putting anything in. And then all of the sudden, the pool is empty. The ability to absorb change had pretty much reached maximum.

Understanding *Values* was critical to help everyone understand there was a need to *really* consider the cross-company blueprints (enterprise architecture)— the absence of which in the end had been blocking previous change attempts.

Interview #2: *A change agent is charged with rationalizing the acquisition of many businesses through the device of information systems. In this process, it's unveiled that an early focus on IT obscured and ignored the difference in Value Systems across the many constituent units. VPEC-T is brought in, but not before some ill-conceived projects are scrapped at great expense.*

DW: You've been sent in to work on a project at a very large organization, which has been through a lot of acquisitions over the years. The parent company gave you the mission of integrating the various operating companies that they'd acquired, which are companies that are basically in the same industry space. What was the main challenge?

AP: Our challenge was to deal with the results of acquiring and being acquired by companies that are in the space, all trying to figure out how they should be working as a single organization providing services to global and local markets.

DW: So the challenge was: in the face of a long series of acquisitions, how can you then get a bunch of businesses that had been operating separately to operate in a more integrated fashion, in order to increase their effectiveness and productivity?

AP: Exactly.

DW: And what were the IT implications of that?

AP: We had initial attempts to go through the integration, happening at a number of different levels, physically on the ground. We asked questions like, "Can we leverage the same facilities? Can we put customer services from different organizations together, selling similar but different products, into the same call centers?" And, of course, it was a similar story with the sales force.

I think IT initially took a rather head-on approach to this. The IT people's mindset was, "We need to provide new solutions." And what we were finding was that every time we went into a geographical business unit, we had to adapt our new solutions to their specific environment. And so we were starting to build huge systems that were trying to address the superset of all the business-unit requirements.

This produced a number of significant failures, where typically in the first business unit we hit, even by way of trying to address just the first business unit's requirements, we ran up against some brick walls. Some of the brick walls were the more traditional project-management type issues you find in the IT environment, and some were more related to the complexity of the environment that we were presented with.

DW: Can you give me an example of a brick wall you ran into in the IT environment?

AP: As we began an implementation project in the finance area, with a well-known ERP [Enterprise Resource Planning] finance package, as soon as the package name was mentioned, it was automatically assumed that the project was an IT project, and not actually a business-transformation project.

So everything's handed over to IT. And they said, "We're going to roll out this package, and there's no need to realign business processes."

DW: This sounds like a classic example of a project being driven from the start by an IT focus—the focus is on "how" rather than "what."

AP: Exactly. The first faulty assumption was that we were talking about a "how" and not a "what." The second faulty assumption was that, because a particular business function seemed to be the recipient of said ERP system, it was just assumed that the changes needed to be made purely in that business function area. And the processes that crossed over from other parts of the business into that functional area weren't exposed at the start of the project, when they should have been.

DW: So you didn't have the *Value Systems* discussion in VPEC-T language.

AP: Exactly. There was no understanding of the Value System. It was a solution for finance, and that was it.

DW: And then you saw the typical failures that result from that—the IT systems were delivered and they didn't meet the needs, they didn't give the perceived value, and then IT's problem-solving reputation dropped.

AP: Absolutely. Even within the IT community running a project like this, they assume most of the development activity was around configuring the off-the-shelf ERP package, and it was a big surprise that, in fact, the bulk of the development work should have actually been in integrating the package with the surrounding environment to enable the *Value System* processes to engage.

Suddenly, very late in the project cycle, we find that we have to do a lot of work to enable interfaces between systems to enable the processes.

Because of this classic behavior in terms of "IT projects," we saw some pretty expensive absolute failures—i.e., projects were scrapped.

DW: What went wrong, in your opinion?

AP: There were a number of reasons. It's important to set the project up with the right levels of accountability for delivery, making sure that when you've got multiple parties involved, you understand who is accountable for what, on one level.

It's also vital to make sure the boundaries are understood and scoped out, and when change comes along, as it always does, make sure that change is understood in context of the original scope.

DW: So, it feels to me that, as IT practitioners, there was some kind of collective memory loss somewhere. I mean, weren't all of those mistakes made years ago?

AP: Yes, absolutely. This is a result of going through acquisition. You do lose memory. Suddenly, the organization has grown dramatically. Everybody has their good ideas of how you should be doing IT, and the best practices don't necessarily shine through in the first instance. *Values* help shine the light on what people want to achieve—and how these objectives are connected (or not!)

Interview #3: *VPEC-T is used to root out the differences in Values between multiple business units in a global organization, and when it was shown how these differing Values informed very different processes in each constituency, a major ERP package was not deployed as a result.*

DW: You're in an organization where the global CIO was considering adopting an IT strategy developed by one division and was planning to apply it worldwide. The IT strategy is based on a standardization agenda enabled by a single vendor of enterprise business software. So what's the problem? Isn't that efficient?

AP: Understandably, this was an appealing strategy. However, it was felt this might not deliver the intended outcomes the business needed in all divisions and business units.

The complication was, when you looked at the face of it, the business was actually doing the same things in all divisions. So, while it was felt the IT strategy wasn't quite right, it was hard to say exactly why. Clearly, getting this decision wrong could have long-lasting negative effects—so we were facing a real dilemma.

DW: Sounds like a big problem. So where does VPEC-T come in?

AP: The first thing that we started talking about was *Values* and *Value Systems*, via VPEC-T.

In order for us come to grips with the difference in Values, we would have to model the business in a different way than had been done previously.

We couldn't use process-modeling techniques, because we knew they didn't surface the real differences. If we mapped a given process, it would kind of look the same across every business unit. So we had to tease out what those differences were—if indeed there were any, of course.

Because we started thinking about *Values*, we thought in a much bigger way about *Values* and *Value Systems*, and what they might be in the context of an individual business unit. And we started by working back to, where was our organization a few years ago, and how has it grown so dramatically in that period of time?

Well, because it had grown through a huge mergers-and-acquisitions program, it had inherited a lot of small businesses.

Many of those companies were businesses with a local geographical business-unit focus. All of those small companies had come with a set of *Values* that they worked to, a set of *goals*, *beliefs*, and, indeed, a set of *Policies* that they operated under, because they were mature, existing businesses.

DW:　　　Sounds like there was a lot of baggage—a lot of history—at the organization that had to be sorted through.

AP:　　　Exactly—the organization had initiated a process of trying to integrate the business, but really, it was done from the marketing point of view—what we jokingly called, "integration by giving everyone the same badge."

The problem was that there was a push toward trying to call *everything* something consistent without actually looking at the underlying *meaning* of things.

Through a series of *workshops* and *interviews* we found out that many of the business units actually functioned in a completely different way. Their operating models were different.

Those differences fundamentally changed the *Value Systems*, changed the way they measured success, changed the way their IT systems were implemented, and changed the way they rewarded companies and individuals within the business ecosystem.

DW: So, understanding *Values* in the VPEC-T dimensional table was what happened first. And it sounds as if you learned something new about the companies that made up the organization that you would not have learned if you had not used VPEC-T.

AP: Yeah, it's interesting. Of course, what I've just described sounds so obvious—and I guess that's the point. But I can tell you, all of those dimensions would have been lost if we had just tried to map a process. We might have identified that there were different players along the process, but really, we would have seen the processes as being the same.

Policies

Interview #4: *The Policies of a global business differ from those of its regional subsidiaries. Application of VPEC-T reveals that, surprisingly, the business does not have a consistent terminology for its moving parts—a serious "loss in translation."*

DW: I understand you're working in a complex global organization embarking on a long-term business transformation. Rather than go for process mapping as the start point, you've been using VPEC-T. Have you learned something new about the business units

| | that make up your organization that you would not have learned if you had not used VPEC-T? |

AP: All of the VPEC-T dimensions would have been lost if we had just tried to map a process. We might have identified that there were different players along the process, but really, we would have seen the processes as being the same. So VPEC-T helped us understand our *starting* point.

DW: What specifically sprung out at you?

AP: We had some interesting insights in terms of Policies. We found that we had to recognize that there were two major different Policies, or policy categories, in play. These were the Policies of the *global* business, which were largely determined and regulated by *external* forces. Many of the policies were standards that were derived from the International Standards Organization (ISO), or from other formal bodies that set up international trade.

So, in other words, the organization didn't necessarily determine all of its policies for its international business. It was kind of told what to do by the regulations.

What's interesting here is that this external policy dimension actually made it much easier to automate the processes and standardize the processes, because they were constrained—or if you like, more fundamentally enabled—by these external rules.

However, when we looked to the businesses in each geographical business unit, of course, there were different *Policies* and regulations.

Even the way we identify simple things like "location" is very different in each geographical business unit's terminology, but when working globally, "location" can be identified by the agreed standard.

We've got these differences that are fundamental in the *Value System*. We've got fundamental differences in *Policies*. Remember, right now we haven't spoken at all about IT.

DW: But you *are* talking about an Information System. And that must have led you on to more discoveries.

AP: Precisely.

The thing that we recognized—and this was a big "a-ha!" moment from a global workshop—was that the number-one issue for all of the geographical business-unit heads represented there was *language*. By language, I mean "business terminology," not "English vs. Spanish." We identified very early on that there was no consistent use of language, particularly around defining a service within a business unit. Contrast this with international standards, which influence common policy and language for the global business.

So this business language had been clouding a number of issues. The operating models seemed to be hiding behind this very simplistic service language. And there are various terms that are used interchangeably, and yet are incredibly different when looked at more closely. The number one problem was a *loss in translation*.

That translation loss was happening because of the varying standards, the varying *Policies*, the varying *Value Systems*, etc. And specifically, when we actually did look at the technology, there was confusion around what the technology actually was. We couldn't really find an easy way to come up with a common way of describing the various line-of-business applications that we had by business function, because things didn't fit in neat boxes.

In fact, we found that, quite often, two things might have had the same name, but were actually very different things.

We'd all been assuming we'd been speaking the same business language in each geographical business unit. But we hadn't. Where policy wasn't informed by a common factor—e.g., an external international standard—the resulting language wasn't common, either. Without VPEC-T this would have been missed. I've talked to friends in other companies, and it turns out this is a really common problem. Obvious, and yet at the same time obscured by assumption.

Events and Content

Interview #5: *A global business whose survival is dependent upon efficient movement of packages realizes it is highly Event-centric. This realization keeps the discussion of a 10-year global business and IT strategy at a high level—and everyone's head above water.*

DW: You're in the process with this company of defining the 10-year vision for global business and IT strategy. Where do *Events* come in to this?

AP: Interestingly enough, one of the key areas where all business units agree—all of the geographical business units agreed, and they also agreed with International—to the point that it was almost a rallying call: "Hooray, we've got something we all agree on!"—was *Events*. And those are specifically the Events around the package movement, the tracking and "When is the package going to arrive and what happens if it didn't arrive? What are the exceptional Events, and how do we process those?"

DW: So is there a course of action that can be taken when you do find that one of the dimensions is not a problem area, but is in fact a point of agreement?

AP: In terms of guiding the global IT strategy, we are focusing on the standards and *Policies* around those *Events*. It was decidedly *not* about implementing a particular software model or something like that, or whether it should be written in Java. We don't care.

DW: The key was to make sure that you understood all the implications of each dimension that was working well, as well as those that were working poorly, and how they affected one another, before you worried about attacking the problems with software.

AP: Right—and what is interesting about the company was that Events made for a relatively easy discussion; because of the nature of its business agreements, the constituent companies shared in their Event-based thinking. The nature of tracking systems is Event-based. If you went into a different organization, or government, for example, they're very immature in their Event-based thinking. And that's why they might have a much richer discussion in that area.

Interview #6: *Thinking about Events and Content, instead of request-supply services and batch processing, averted the creation of an extremely unwieldy and outdated IT infrastructure.*

DW: You're helping a global business define a strategy for transformation. Let's talk a little about how Events and Content played into the strategic thinking.

AP: This may sound a little strange, but Events and Content were undeniably the most successful parts of the strategy definition.

The company had started down a way of thinking about what they were going to do next in terms of "request-supply" services. And we got them to think in terms of Events, rather than in terms of "request-supply services," which we didn't think was very helpful. We thought it was more helpful to think in terms of significant business Events.

It immediately made their multi-channel strategy much more amenable to analysis.

For example, the most confusing example for the company was concerning the accounts engine, which holds all the balances by account. The payment engine needs to see those balances to make its payment decision. Therefore, we need a request-supply service from payments to the accounts engine so that it can look at every one of those accounts. We might also need a request-supply service in the accounts engine if the payment engine's asking it to make a decision.

Now if we'd implemented that, every single financial transaction in the accounts engine could have involved the accounts engine calling the payments engine, which would then call the accounts engine back repeatedly.

If that really was what we were going to do, that would have been a nonsense business process and IT architecture.

DW: So, in other words, there would have been some really complex business processes?

AP: Yes. Basically, every process and system would become extremely flaky, and if one component wasn't in place, or was changed, nothing would work. And it would have been an extremely latent system, because the system that otherwise could have looked at all that data immediately ends up waiting for it to go across the network 20 times. And there was no business reason for doing things this way.

So we got the company to think in terms of Events and Content, and how they interrelate. The solution to this problem is, if both the accounts engine and the payment engine need to see balances, then they had both better have balances. What that means is, every time a balance changes, which is a business Event, that Event should be sent to both engines. And they can do with them what they need to do in order to be able to do their work.

This became a very general principle in what we were discussing: Every time they were thinking in terms of request-supply services, we asked them to define the Content they were missing, and then find the business Event that gets them that Content.

This became, if you like, a whole new business philosophy to inform the strategy for transformation.

DW: It sounds analogous to having a conference call as a business Event, rather than all of the concerned individuals calling each other repeatedly, trying to get one piece of information.

AP: Right, and I think the benefit was actually about how you decouple stuff within the business and

IT architecture much more effectively than you would do if you did so through a request-supply schema.

The other effect is that it gets the company back to thinking in terms of the *business*, what data is in the *business*, what the Content *is*, and what business Events it services, rather than thinking in terms of something that's really very cobbled together.

If you think in terms of request-supply routines, you could have as many as you like. You could have a request-supply for, "how many red-headed customers from Springfield do we have?" It's not a business-meaningful thing. It's whatever somebody wants to ask.

DW: This is kind of about business plumbing—the problem was that the company was talking about the "how" rather than the "what," right? It's a kind of an abstract plumbing discussion, isn't it?

AP: Right, and when you are *only* talking about plumbing, you're probably going to end up doing the plumbing wrong, if you have that discussion that way.

You'll find that there are a lot of ingrained attitudes in IT, and you can trace them back to not thinking in terms of VPEC-T. Once you get IT and business personnel thinking in terms of Values and the context level, and what's changing in the Values, the practitioners understand that "*we* have to reorganize." Once they start thinking that way, it's a completely different discussion than, "The *business says* we have to reorganize." Now they start to understand *why*, and why that means that certain things they thought were important before no longer are important, and things they thought were unimportant before now are very important.

So that's how we established the Values dimension. The Policies and Trust dimensions are all about IT people acting on behalf of their business colleagues, and the need to get intimate with both camps and set up these Trust relationships.

Events and Content then answer the question, "what is the truth of the business you're doing?" And the answer is not "in the happenstance way it's currently implemented," but is in fact another question: "what is it to provide quality service on our accounts?"

DW: So it sounds as if this implementation of VPEC-T was about helping the client ask the right question, because they were fundamentally asking the wrong question, and therefore coming up with the wrong answer.

AP: Absolutely. To give you an example of that, the company is very used to doing an awful lot of stuff in batch-processing format. There's no business reason for doing the vast majority of their processing in batches. A lot of it is done in batch just because "that's the way it was always done." Once we started asking questions about Event and Content, they started to realize, "We can't show you that Event, because actually it's part of a whole bunch of things that happen at night." And we said, "Well, why does that happen at night? How can you set up these Trust relationships and perform tasks on behalf of the business owner if everything is being condensed into one big blob of batch processing at night?" And the answer is, of course, you can't.

There are some business Events that occur inherently overnight. Summing up a set of funds and coming up with a fund value is a business Event that occurs overnight. But the fact of it is, it should be treated as a business Event, and one you have to take care of and understand what to do with.

In IT terms, this batch process is a technical solution to a problem that no longer exists, which was: limited network bandwidth, limited disk sizes, slow CPUs, and poor storage. A lot of the reasons why you did things overnight in batches are gone.

DW: So, what VPEC-T recognizes is that technology now allows us to create information systems and use information technology that is a much better simulation of reality, or reflection of reality, than we've had before.

AP: VPEC-T is just really another way of talking about realities that have existed since the beginning of time. We haven't had the language, because we kind of bent it all around things like batch processes, and the development of the technology, and as a result we've been constrained by these distortions, which are a consequence of fascination with the technology, to the exclusion of understanding the business reasons for the technology.

This example illustrates that the way in which people analyze the business today—and specifically systems of the business—is too myopic. They take too narrow a focus, because the tools they have makes them take a narrow focus. And when you use VPEC-T, it broadens the number of dimensions you use to actually analyze the problem.

DW: You analyze the problem in terms of the truth of the real world.

AP: Right. What was most ironic was that it had already occurred to the company that the best way to analyze the original accounts system, which was built in 1984, was at first to use VPEC-T. But it turns out that the basic mid-1980s view of accounting was of an online system that records business Events and uses them to keep a set of balances updated. It then shifts the Events to an overnight process that creates Content in the form of new balances, and shifts the Content back to the online system so it can start again the next day.

Once they realized that's actually how their systems worked, and that the only thing they're doing differently now is keeping exactly the same view of Events and Content, but in real time, they certainly felt much more confident about what we were doing. They started to realize what had gone wrong and how it could be fixed.

Trust

Interview #7: *Once Values are discovered at a highly federated, global organization during a business-transformation project, issues of Trust are then bridged. The key is seeing IT solution adoption as the result of a "pull" that speaks to everyone's role in an Information System, rather than something that is simply "pushed" out by the leadership and humbly accepted by the plebiscite.*

DW Like most organizations, you've had a bunch of painful experiences. And you wanted to think about things in a different way. What did you think of VPEC-T when you originally encountered it, and then how did you put it to work?

AP: I had actually taken on a project last year within the organization, which involved using some of the principles of VPEC-T, but not necessarily all of them. Some of those principles are now beginning to be applied in the full execution of that particular project, which is a very sizeable business transformation.

DW: Which of the principles do you think were the most significant in that project?

AP: One of the critical principles was *Trust*. We're in a very highly federated organization, where typically the business-unit general manager is king. They have a P&L that they have to manage, and there's not necessarily a high degree of Trust between them and group management, who, in the view of the business-unit management, typically comes along and makes their life difficult by asking them to implement new systems, new processes, etc. Of course, everyone's trying to do the right thing within their own units or group perspectives. But from the business-unit perspective, group activity is often seen as a "push out from the center," rather than a pull from the business unit. So one of the fundamental things that we've had to do is build Trust between the center and group.

DW: How have you been building that Trust?

AP: By constant collaboration and communication. That means not just creating things and then just pushing them over the fence. That collaboration is arrived at by building a common set of *Values*, making sure that we all understand what it is that's driving us as an organization, and what needs to be fixed. And in a federated organization that needs to work together to deliver the customer service, that's all about establishing an understanding of what it is to be a part of the end-to-end service delivery, understanding that you're no longer just a king in your own geographical business unit, but that you're reliant on other geographical business units and the group, to be able to perform your business, and vice versa. They're dependent on you.

DW: So another way of putting that is, "When we look at the world through an IT practitioner's lens, it's about really understanding that you're a member of an information system."

AP: Yes, at one level, but it actually goes a level beyond that. In information-system terms, it's about actually having information available to you to do your job. You will not only be measured by your P&L, your financial bottom line, and your operational performance, but on your *information* performance as well.

In other words, "Am I provided the information I need, and am I receiving the information I need on time, to the quality I expect?" It's understanding that "the group can't survive without me, and I can't survive without the group" at the information-systems level.

Interview #8:   *The Business/IT divide is narrowed when an organization realizes that projects go much more smoothly when there is a business owner who is uniquely responsible for each of them, and when IT solutions are not seen as being the sole province of IT practitioners. But first Trust has to be established, and then Policies created in view of that Trust, before the gap truly closes.*

DW: You've been working some time now with the major global organization providing leadership in the business-IT divide. What are some of the big issues that you see as causing the divide, and where does VPEC-T come in?

AP: One of the reasons I think there was a problem between business and IT at the company revolved around this whole question of *Policies* and *Trust*. The IT organization had built systems as though they were owned by IT, even though they really were owned by the business. And therefore, they'd never really had to explore the Trust issues between elements of the business, because they always said, "We own all that on your behalf."

That attitude didn't scale. That was holding us back and stopping us from being able to do things for the business. The one part of IT that didn't do this, and was considered to be the only successful part of IT, had a much more intimate relationship with its business partners, and did indeed put *Trust* into its relationship with the other parts of the business.

DW: Did you try to say, "Look at what this division is doing"?

AP: We did do that—this turned out to be a very contentious issue for the IT people, and particularly the IT management. It suddenly became obvious that the concept of *Trust* was limiting what they could and couldn't do. It was a constraint they hadn't realized they had. And it also directly affected their relationship to the business, and what the business could and couldn't do.

In the beginning of the engagement the sense was, "Well, we don't understand what you're talking about." In the middle of the engagement it was, "We don't want you to talk about this." And at the end of the engagement it was, "This is our key message to the management."

DW: The IT people came back with a plan after initially refusing discussion? Where was the business side in their transformation?

AP: It was like, the three phases of fascination, denial, and acceptance for IT.

The business has already gone down this path. They've gone down this path themselves for a couple of reasons, though. One of the side effects of Sarbanes-Oxley is that it forces the business to address some of these issues. Sarbanes-Oxley says, "Every business system must have one unequivocal business owner who's prepared to sign off on it." So that business owner definitively says, "If I'm going to sign off on this, it's mine."

So now, systems which were run on behalf of those business owners by IT as a whole now have to be clearly separated, one from the other, and the way you do that separation is by setting up *Trust*.

The key thing is, you say, "if these two different business systems have to communicate and they have different business owners, then we must set up an arrangement by which that can happen, which is the *Policy*." So we explained to them that they needed a whole bunch of Policies that they didn't have, and

Trust relationships that they hadn't yet created. It became very contentious.

Interview #9: *VPEC-T isn't only for IT issues. In this case, pursuing a better understanding of Values and Trust helped guide the office of the CEO to a new business strategy and corporate governance model.*

DW: You're working in a project to help the CEO office determine its future business strategy and corporate governance model. How has VPEC-T helped?

AP: VPEC-T really helped us focus on a new set of *Values* discussions—but through an improved understanding of *Trust* relationships.

DW: What do you mean?

AP: We started to talk about the Value System of the global corporation in terms of mergers, acquisitions, and divestments. Do we want to buy more companies? Should we invest in them?

We then had the flip discussion at a business-unit level, which said, "what are you doing, what have you got, let's see if you've got any best practices down there, and is there anything that you might want to share with your other business-unit colleagues?"

Like most organizations, our geographical business units are grouped into divisions. This gave us a third dimension of the *Values* discussion, where each division wanted to its own thing, as it believed this to be in the best interest of both business units and group.

So there are three very different things going on here.

But they're all part of the same discussion today, all part of the same topic, which is, everyone saying, "This is all about a shared strategy."

The business units are saying, "Look, I need some direction from the divisional office and from Global to tell me what to do. Because I'm being told I'm not going to get my needed investments unless I comply with a strategy. But you're telling me there isn't a strategy, so how the heck do I comply with it?"

And the CEO is saying, "Hang on a minute. I still want this answer about whether I should invest in these businesses or divest. So what are you doing, guys?"

And then we've got another bunch of people saying, "I don't know why you're bothering with these divisional guys who are arguing about strategy, because we've already done it on our division, and they should implement what we've done."

So we had to go through some fairly soul-searching discussions that really allowed us to express very clearly, in very simple terms, what the issues were, how we could talk about these Value Systems, how we could talk about the language, and how we could actually talk about the emerging *Trust* issues that were surfacing.

DW: And that's how you arrived at the Trust dimension…

AP: Right, because we had *Trust* relationship issues between the geographical business units and the divisions, and the divisions and group.

We had this really complex sort of dynamic, and a number of what we call *tension points* surfaced. And when you've got tension points, you've got to do something about that. You have to decide whether you're going to tolerate, negotiate, innovate, or escalate them. We found that, by understanding and discussing the tension points head on, we are now engaging in a genuine shared effort for a genuine shared business strategy.

Thinking about VPEC-T in Combination

Interview #10:   *In order to maintain its position as number one in its headquarters nation, a financial-services company in the throes of a business-transformation project deployed every dimension of VPEC-T in its quest to expand and stay competitive.*

DW: It definitely seems like using VPEC-T aligns you better with your business goals.

AP: It makes you go back and revisit the business goals under a new lens. It makes you realize things can change from where they were 20 years ago.

This is actually enabling business transformation to occur, when, before, looking at it through a technology lens, it was actually impeding business transformation.

DW: Why was the business doing this transformation?

AP: They stated that relatively clearly. They said, "We need to maintain our position as number one in our headquarters nation, and we need to expand into new geographies to increase market share. This is the only way we are going to stay in business."

DW: So there was a real sense of urgency?

AP: The way it was put to me was, "Unless we get this going and get it going fast, this company will be taken over and none of us will have jobs. It's crucial for our survival as an independent entity." They needed to get themselves into a leading position, where they were getting their costs way down by not duplicating things and doing things in the most expensive way possible, and get their agility up, so they could compete in new geographies, in order to become an expanding company. If they don't do that, they will be acquired.

DW: So in other words, VPEC-T can solve mission-critical problems, not just bridge the gap between business and IT.

AP: Yes.

DW: It seems we've visited all of the VPEC-T dimensions. When you execute VPEC-T, does it always happen in that sequence, starting with Values and ending with Trust?

AP: You can start anywhere in the thread. You could start talking about Trust, and you get to the other dimensions. You could start talking about Events, and get to Values, etc.

I live in a business context, so when you're looking at a business problem, you would generally tend to start with Values.

If you're in the technology world, where you're looking at issues around making some of these more practical things work, quite often you start at Events.

When you're looking at some of the more abstract things, like establishing an enterprise governance process, it's the *Value Systems* that steer you to some of the early issues that you're going to find.

So the real answer is, it depends where you start and the problem you're trying to solve.

There is no cookbook. We don't want to pretend there's a cookbook. This is a thinking framework, and thus it requires you to think.

DW: So VPEC-T is giving you a set of dimensions by which you look at a problem?

AP: Yeah, one of the early judgments you're making is, "Which of those dimensions are valid to building a cogent argument around the area that you want to discuss?"

It's a way of remembering the important things to think about.

If you're doing an engagement and you're talking about Events a lot, then it forces you to ask, "Why haven't I talked about Content?" And if you talk about Events and Content, you say, "Why didn't Policies and Trust come up? What's missing?"

And then in all cases, you're not going to get change unless the context is changed—and that's all about Values.

DW: There's no particular order in which the VPEC-T dimensions need to be covered. They just need to be kept in mind.

AP: Absolutely. You may actually look at some of the dimensions and say, "Actually, I don't need to discuss that, because it's not relevant to the argument."

VPEC-T is a thinking framework. But if you think of it only in terms of that sequence of letters, it appears to be a cookbook. It's not a cookbook.

Interview #11: *The global company that exposed its Value System differences in order to avert IT-deployment disaster now must grapple with Policies, Events, Content and Trust, and in so doing, will move away from reflexively thinking about technology before it considers the higher-level needs that drive IT adoption.*

DW: What are the next steps? What do you consider the pay-off of applying VPEC-T at this global company?

AP: We're now at the point where there's a much clearer understanding of what we're dealing with. We're understanding all these *Value Systems*. We can expect them. We have some ways of resolving the *tension points*. We aren't there yet, but we know that they are on the list of things to do.

We've moved away from a focus on technology. We're not talking about, "we'll take this great practice, this great piece of software from business unit A, and deploy it in business unit B." It's not as simple as that. There's work we have to do first.

When we get that work done, then there needs to be work done around standards, which actually leads to an IS architecture.

An IS architecture is where we start the journey of joining the *Information Systems* to the information technology. The whole point of it is to join the Information systems and business view with the technology view.

DW: How do VPEC-T, information systems and systems thinking relate?

AP: The problem that we found, and the reason why VPEC-T thinking is proving so useful, was that systems thinking was still in the domain of the "nerd." It still wasn't rich enough.

Now, with the VPEC-T dimensions, we now have the basis for a much, much more meaningful discussion around information-systems architecture, which may lead to a much more informed, intelligent, adoptable, and cost-effective IT architecture.

So in this case, the VPEC-T creates the much richer starting point for this architecture work, and then the rest is proven down the road, in that you get the systems, and you don't have project-cost overruns, and so forth.

DW: What would you say is the payoff directly for the company bottom line?

AP: We know we've avoided a very, very costly mistake. A global project that had cost the company millions was thrown away before it was deployed in even the second business unit, because we realized that we had not done this work; we had not had the VPEC-T discussion. VPEC-T has already saved the company several hundreds of millions of dollars.

DW: How will you continue to deploy VPEC-T at the company?

AP: It is there when I approach any particular problem within the project. For example, there is the problem of how to classify and rate best-practice solutions from around the group. I think about a list of criteria to judge the reusability of a best-practice solution, and I'm thinking, "How do I classify the Value System in the business unit of origin? What is its scope in terms of *Policies, Events* and *Content*? What might the Trust system relationships be, or not be, that might prohibit or preclude a best-practice solution from being reused outside its business unit of origin?"

DW: How is VPEC-T more than just a technology solution?

AP: VPEC-T really shines in this example around the topic of *reuse*. The things that seem to be more important than the basic IT assessment of "best practice," are in fact the *Value Systems* in the originating business unit, and those operating in any potential source business units.

The barriers to adoption are relatively few when you look at the more technical criteria. But the barriers are legion when you look at the VPEC-T dimensions.

Once those Value Systems are better understood, new opportunities open up.

If the company were to be frank with itself, would it consider the reuse of a system built by one of its smaller organizations in-house with a small IT capability, as opposed to reusing an international package built by one of its bigger organizations with maturity in software development, or via partner arrangement if it's a third-party product? That's the kind of discussion that we're having.

DW: Right. But you're saying that in some cases, a smaller system that would not normally have been considered as the source of a best practice could actually be considered for wider adoption.

AP: Yeah, but then we're looking at things in terms of, to what degree of reusability are we discussing "best practice?" Are we looking at the *pattern* that has been employed, and if so, do we reuse the design, in which case, does that design lend itself to the Value Systems of potential targets? Or are we talking about implementing the actual *solution*, and if so, who's going to provide support for that ongoing management and maintenance? And then we run into the *Trust* issue.

DW: Is there an advantage to adding VPEC-T early in the discussion?

AP: I think it provides for a richer analysis of both current and future potential situations. As an IT architect, I really wouldn't be interested too much in *Value Systems* or *Trust* in particular. I'd probably be a bit more interested in *Policies*, *Content* and *Events*, but I'd probably be expressing them from an IT perspective, rather than a business perspective. So, bringing these issues in upfront gives us a richer set of information from which to develop judgments and recommendations.

Without that information set, I think you increase your risk of being IT-led, and therefore increasing your chances of failing in terms of business-IT alignment.

The concepts of VPEC-T provide our business Content. Therefore, they simplify the dialogue IT has with the business. You're immediately forced into talking in the business' terms.

When you look at something in the cold light of its IT life, you really miss the point about its context and what it has been built to respond to. Because, ultimately, the information system is a response to a set of needs that are driven by the *Value System* in the business unit that we're talking about. And that Value System is expressed quite well through VPEC-T.

DW: I can see how VPEC-T helps the people directly involved and the company as a whole, but how do you make that clear to management who may not be involved directly?

AP: VPEC-T provides practitioners the ability to put together pretty succinct statements around some pretty complex issues.

For example, the stock-take that was done for one client was very much bottom-up: "Tell me all about what you've got in your business unit in the form of information systems and information technology." But it was informed by our VPEC-T thinking, because a top-down analysis was also informed by VPEC-T thinking. So then the two meet in the middle. Then we've got an in-built alignment of terms and terminology, around which we can express Content.

That manifests itself in the quality of the report back to senior management. If you're in the general management board, you don't care that there are 140 Visual Basic applications used in finance. What I care about if I'm the general management board is, "Are there any major investment needs within the finance domain that might be suitably met by an information system or a pattern for an information system in a

DW: What are the next steps for VPEC-T at the company?

AP: We're starting now to set out some of the key steps forward in a number of dimensions, particularly around the progression from information standards at the local level, through shared information standards within the overall network, with the ultimate result being a global application portfolio.

There are some serious adoption issues involved in moving from one step to the next, based particularly on the *Value System* of the business units that we're asking to take the journey. And it would be that much more of an arduous journey, and many points would have been missed, if we did not have VPEC-T at our disposal.

DW Is it fair to say most businesses already have elements of VPEC-T in their organization?

AP: I'm thinking about successful projects in the past, and of instances of failure. And I would generally say that things that have really succeeded do exhibit the various aspects of VPEC-T, with Trust being the ultimate result, in a way. The things that have failed may have had one or two of the elements, but certainly not all of the elements.

Interview #12: *VPEC-T helps organizations revolutionize their thinking—by acknowledging and grappling with complexity, rather than attempting to boil it down into processes. It helps practitioners see more clearly the aspects that must change, and just as importantly,* *the aspects that are working well and are left well enough alone.*

DW: How has VPEC-T helped your company reduce business complexity?

AP: You can't fix everything overnight. And maybe you actually don't need to fix everything. I work in the business context. From an IT side, there does seem to be a tendency to say, from an IT standpoint—and it's not necessarily IT that puts this forth—"if we are performing the same processes, why can't we use the same systems? Therefore, we should be rolling out the same systems."

DW: And a big part of your job was to disabuse people of that kind of thinking.

AP: Exactly. I think we had a number of interviews with business-unit SVPs, and the very first interview we conducted in order to understand their environment got the reaction: "I don't know why you're talking about processes or looking at processes, because you won't understand the differences by looking at processes until you look at the detail of the processes."

What you need to look at is other dimensions. And as it turns out, some of those dimensions, or most of the dimensions, appear to be VPEC-T dimensions.

DW: As you went through this, was there a point where you realized, "Hey, everybody, it's VPEC-T, that's what we've been doing!" There was no "A-ha!" moment like that?

AP: No. But what we've discovered, working in this environment, is that it's actually better to use things like VPEC-T as a frame of reference for the practitioners, and not necessarily to relay these terms to the subject matter experts, as it were. It's better to use these things as devices, to illustrate what we're actually going through.

DW: So, VPEC-T is not implemented like other approaches that have been marketed to management, where the business leaders impose a system from above and instruct their employees to implement it.

AP: Certainly not at the moment. Because what you're grappling with is, at the end of the day, an attempt to understand complexity. And people have a tendency to try and simplify things, and then they use their own models for doing that. The dimension that seems to gel, certainly with people in this organization, is **process.** As I just mentioned, in a way, process oversimplifies things to a degree that everything looks the same. And it can actually lose the differences that you're trying to expose.

DW: And it's important to make sure you acknowledge where those differences exist, and try not to pave over them with a single system as a response.

AP: Exactly.

DW: We've talked about making the organization responsive to itself, but how do you transmit VPEC-T values to the customers? Do you think it's becoming clear to the end user yet?

AP: It's too early in the cycle to say, however, I did receive some anecdotal evidence just today that some customers are actually being engaged even at this early stage. They understand what we're doing, because there is already an element of Trust.

VPEC-T History and Bibliography

The Birth of VPEC-T

An interview with the Authors

The story of VPEC-T began in 2005 when the authors were part of a team working with a large federated organization undertaking a business transformation program to 'join-up' and share business information more effectively. Soon, it became clear that the challenges the team had surfaced would become the foundation for VPEC-T, a framework that is applicable across almost any type of organization.

Interviewer: Dan Woods (DW)

Interviewees: Nigel Green (NG)

                Carl Bate (CB)

DW: I understand VPEC-T was born out of a business transformation program with a large-scale information sharing aspect to it. Can you tell me how and why you first thought of it?

CB: Quite early into this endeavor, Nigel and I were walking along the street after work one evening, and we said, "Isn't it funny how we're seeing that the patterns of the Web seem to be really helpful here? We're seeing the patterns of the supply-chain industry being very helpful as well. But everyone around us is focusing on the process, and the data, and nobody seems to be talking about Policies, Events, and Content." At the end of that conversation, I distinctly remember we came up with those three words.

NG: We were recognizing that there were these conflicting discussions going on, although we hadn't thought specifically to give them the label of "Values" or "Value System." We just thought, "Well, there are all these people fighting, and that's having an effect on what we're trying to do here." At that moment in time, I thought we had a real breakthrough just by defining PEC = policies, events, and content.

CB: And we said, "Isn't it funny PEC could be an extremely useful way to describe all information?"

"If everything's a P, E, or a C, then you can have descriptions of what the data is, and then you have the data itself—that could be really powerful. We're 'un-thinking' this concept of process and data, of function and data, which connects P and C together, sometimes in a very unhelpful way, which means people can't cooperate."

NG: And then we recognized that dealing with the conflicting values had been such a crucial part of the project so far—hence we added the V to PEC.

DW: When did the "-T" in VPEC-T come in?

NG: Well, the "-T" came to life in a number of ways. The first way was a job we worked on that involved security and privacy domains.

When we were looking at the various security issues across data-privacy domains, we saw this lack of Trust because of the different Value Systems of some very traditional and long-established fiefdoms. These fiefdoms actually existed within business units, as well as across business units. We had this huge paradox of being directed by top-down policy that these units must share, and we were there to help them share. And yet, none of them wanted to share anything because they didn't really trust each other.

We had to focus on the Trust relationships and work out how we could develop and nurture them.

CB: They say that necessity is the mother of invention. And we were certainly getting inventive!

I think that was the genesis of the PEC dimensions. Nigel then drew up a couple panels to start to tease out some of the PEC thinking, which had been the result of this initial assessment of what was going on.

I also distinctly remember holding a quote in the back of my mind from Tim Berners-Lee where he said "The problem with the Web is that we don't teach, in academic institutions, what the model is really about. We might teach the standards and the technologies, but we don't teach what the model is *about*." I think the reality is many of us, even in the IT industry, think we understand the Web model—but I agree with Tim, I think the understanding is only just surfacing. And boy, were we going to be going deep into the Web model.

One of the things that struck us about externalization was that VPEC-T is a really nice way to describe things that are "external"—to actually work with the Web model. The Web starts with the premise that any information, or any resource, can be used by any person or machine, for any purpose. The Corporate IT, pre-Web model started with the opposite premise: that IT was used by certain people with well-defined constraints, for certain purposes. When you start from the other position, and you actually have these VPEC-T dimensions to think about IT in that world, it actually is not only helpful in the specific situation, it actually helps you start to get your mind around the Web. I've actually found this journey, personally, to be one of a true understanding of what the Web model represents.

NG: That becomes particularly relevant as we move into a Web-driven world where we think about things like "software as a service" and mashups, and finer-grained Web services, and how they're going to be combined. It just fits so well in that framework—by serendipity, it would seem.

CB: Externalization is a connected theme—it's kind of the call to action—it's actually the call to action, the reason and the trend all in one. With these insights front-of-mind, it's really interesting to Nigel and I, as we go about work with colleagues in various situations. As we look at SaaS, or at mashups, or we look at the Semantic Web, or at Ontology, or at business themes around demand versus supply management, VPEC-T and externalization become really useful in understanding what is going on. We think the concepts are helping others to have different types of conversations, which appear to create a better understanding of the realities of a Web-enabled world, and to therefore be better able to achieve their objectives in that world.

DW: I'd like to ask about Trust. Just as differences in Values can result in conflicts, Trust issues can also be a source of conflict. The idea of the Trust dimension is just to recognize, "Okay, we've understood our different Values, we've understood the Policies, Events, and Content, and now we can make a map of what we do around here, and maybe make a new map of what we want to do around here, in terms of V, P, E and C. But if we still don't trust each other, we're going to have a lot of difficulty dealing with that. If we don't trust each other, we have to acknowledge that, and deal with it somehow." Is that the Trust dimension?

NG: Trust is probably actually the biggest dimension of them all, because it has so many different facets. At the highest level, you can think of Trust as community building.

DW: When you first realized these dimensions, what was the mechanism of addressing the Trust issue?

NG: When looking at the Trust issues around information sharing, we sought ways that would help us fully understand them. These issues weren't being discussed. People weren't asking the trust question—it was all too embarrassing. We actually had to call it—our discussions with information providers and consumers went something like this:

        "Well, you know, you said you were going to share with [the other party]. Are you really going to share [subject] information?"

        [*Pregnant pause.*]

        "You don't really trust those guys, do you?"

        "Well, no."

        "So, are you going to share or not?"

        "Well, yeah, well, hmm…"

And so on...

Until the question for all parties involved became, "How do we resolve this?" We started to come up with different suggestions of ways that they could use, for example, multi-channel Policies for sharing information and the use of a mixture of both Content and Events information across multiple channels.

For example, there might be a piece of information that one department really needs, yet the other department doesn't really want to give it to them on a regular basis—or, they may have issues about giving it to each other electronically at all. So rather than actually sending the information on a completely systematic, regular basis, it may be that for the occasion when that information is really needed, an Event is used as a proxy for the content that says, "Somebody really wants this [subject] information."

DW: So, in this example, because this event happened, you all now have permission to see this information.

NG: That's right. You now have the opportunity, as the owner of the content, to release it when you want, and how you want—maybe using a different channel. In some cases, rather than it going as an electronic message or an email or whatever, it might actually be released over the telephone, or it might be delivered verbally in a face-to-face meeting. This takes us back to the idea of a complete information system that includes human-to-human communication. And that could be part of the Trust model needed.

DW: You've said that you think Trust may be the most significant of the dimensions. Do you think the naïve IT approach—that is, answering the "how" when you really want to ask about "what"—destroys Trust with the business? In other words, nobody believes anybody else is there to help or can help.

NG: I think that's a brilliant question. I've never thought of it that way.

DW: You described this state of focusing on the "how" in the absence of all the VPEC-T dimensions. This resulted in an area in which the Trust was so eroded, that people were putting up barriers—they wanted to avoid having to rely on each other.

NG: Yes, particularly when it came to IT. As soon as anybody other than the original IT project owner wanted to do something, they said, "No, you can't do that unless..." They set the Trust hurdle so high that it was impossible to do any work.

DW: It seems that, early on, the question to ask when you are considering VPEC-T might be: "Is your environment one in which, when the IT department comes around, you get a little nervous? You're a little worried that your time is going to be wasted and you're not going to get what you want." It is not a result of the IT department being hateful and nasty. It's a communication problem.

CB: This exact point came up at another of our clients. Because in the industry we don't seem to have sight of PEC dimensions, and we seem to have IT solutions that don't actually respect the business operating model, and they don't seem to be helpful to enforce the policies that we have to enforce—maybe, unfairly, that creates a loss of Trust in the IT department.

DW: So, we could say that VPEC-T allows you to create an environment in which success can restore Trust.

The only thing that restores Trust is success. Through VPEC-T analysis, people are released from their normal reflexive distrust, because this feels different, and they see how they're going to get what they want.

NG: Right. However, it's a journey; it's not an instant, trust-restoring pill.

CB: As we trust each other more, we might declare our Values more honestly to each other. We might actually start saying what it is we really want from the information system, without trying to hide things. We might start to talk about our goals more openly and honestly with each other, and in so doing, we start to help each other out more as well.

DW: With that final bit of food for thought, I'd like to thank you, Carl and Nigel. It was great to hear about the journey and how you discovered the value of thinking VPEC-T.

Books that Particularly Influenced our Thinking

Books of Influence

This bibliography contains some of the more significant books I've read over the past twenty years or so. What struck me about them is how relevant much of the thinking is today. In particular, I've found a recurring resonance between the world of System Thinking, as described by Pirsig and Capra, with the world of the Web. Interestingly, I've found that abstracting up to System Thinking (Chunking Up) has been extremely useful when assessing the impact and potential of Web 2.0/3.0 technologies on the future direction of corporate IT. System Thinking is also useful for looking at both the "softer" interaction and "harder" transaction aspects of an overall Information System.

When I reflect on it, however, the theme that I find most compelling is the importance of human behavior and social norms to Information Systems, in combination with planned and unplanned events. It's worth considering the impact to Information Systems if these aspects are left unexplored; they often become the barriers to the adoption of IT-enabled change, and therefore, a blocker to needed business outcomes.

What I find most interesting is the search for the sweet spot between classical engineering approaches and the early examination of adoption barriers. It seems to me that some of the most successful Web-enabled businesses (the likes of Google, Amazon, and eBay) have used an adoption-led approach to the development of products and services. Corporate IT, in contrast, often continues to take a more traditional approach to "engineering" its way to a solution.

Is this difference in approach where we might wring the long-sought value for the enterprise from the world of the Web? — *Nigel Green*

Fritjof Capra

The work of Fritjof Capra, a world-renowned physicist, further develops the idea of systems thinking and the value of seeking a balance between classic and romantic, right-brain and left-brain, mechanistic and organic, in a contemporary setting. His work embraces the notion of accepting events as they unfold and responding to them in a more natural, behavioral way. He focuses on the relationships between systems and provides deeper insights to cause and effect through his understanding of how things actually work, and through his knowledge of sub-atomic physics, illustrating its similarities to human belief systems. His insights have stimulated our adoption thinking.

Titles:
"The Tao of Physics: An Exploration of the Parallels Between Modern Physics and Eastern Mysticism."
"The Web of Life: A New Scientific Understanding of Living Systems"
"The Turning Point: Science, Society and the Rising Culture"

Claudio Ciborra

Ciborra's focus on Information Systems further explores the nature of information and the effect of human behavior and unfolding events within an information system. His use of the French term *bricolage* encapsulates the notion of end-user empowerment within an information system. He directly challenges conventional wisdom and suggests that top-down, grand design and control are doomed to failure. He points to an alternative center of gravity: human existence in everyday life.

His work helps us develop our thinking around "Shadow IT," end-use adoption, and the impact of an increasingly "Externalized" world.

Title:

"The Labyrinths of Information: Challenging the Wisdom of Systems"

W. Chan Kim & Renee Mauborgne

The collective work of Kim & Mauborgne examines how businesses might create game-changing strategies through a technique called Value Innovation. This work, led by the authors, was developed by economists and other business specialists at the INSEAD and Harvard business schools during the early 2000s. Their focus on markets, and how to shape and respond to them, has informed our thinking around how the subjects of IS and IT could be better addressed—both in long-range planning and day-to-day execution. Moreover, the Value Innovation focus helped us develop our thinking about rigorous alignment with desired business outcomes and being brave enough to challenge market norms.

Title:

"Blue Ocean Strategy: How to Create Uncontested Market Space and Make the Competition Irrelevant"

Robert Pirsig

Foundational to the Values and Trust dimensions of VPEC-T is Pirsig's observation on the meaning of "quality and value" in the context of multiple interacting systems of value, and the way he uses a common framework for describing a wide variety of systems behaviors (biological, economic, social, mechanical, etc.).

Titles:
"Zen and The Art of Motorcycle Maintenance"
"Lila: An Inquiry Into Morals"

A to Z Bibliography

Alexander, Christopher; Ishikawa, Sara; Silverstein, Murray; Jacobson, Max; Fiksdahl-King, Ingrid; Angel, Shlomo. *A Pattern Language: Towns, Buildings, Construction.* New York: Oxford University Press, 1977.

Anderson, Chris. *The Long Tail: Why the Future of Business is Selling Less of More.* New York: Hyperion, 2006.

Brooks, Frederick. *The Mythical Man-Month: Essays on Software Engineering.* Reading, Mass: Addison-Wesley, 1975.

Capra, Fritjof. *The Tao of Physics: An Exploration of the Parallels Between Modern Physics and Eastern Mysticism.* Boston, Mass.: Shambala Publications, 1991.

Capra, Fritjof. *The Turning Point: Science, Society and the Rising Culture.* New York: Simon and Schuster, 1982.

Capra, Fritjof. *The Web of Life: A New Scientific Understanding of Living Systems.* New York: Anchors Books, 1997.

Checkland, Peter; Scholes, Jim. *Soft Systems Methodology in Action.* Chichester, UK: John Wiley & Sons, 1999.

Ciborra, Claudio. *The Labyrinths of Information: Challenging the Wisdom of Systems.* Oxford, UK: Oxford University Press, 2002.

Gladwell, Malcolm. *The Tipping Point: How Little Things Can Make a Big Difference.* Boston, Mass.: Little, Brown, 2000.

Gleick, James. *Chaos: Making a New Science.* New York: Viking, 1987.

Goswami, Amit. *The Self-Aware Universe: How Consciousness Creates the Material World.* New York: Putnam, 1993.

Heinrich, Claus. *RFID and Beyond: Growing Your Business Through Real World Awarness.* Wiley, 2005.

Hoff, Benjamin. *The Tao of Pooh.* New York: E.P. Dutton, 1982.

Kim, W. Chan; Mauborgne, Renee. *Blue Ocean Strategy: How to Create Uncontested Market Space and Make the Competition Irrelevant.* Boston, Mass.: Harvard Business School Press, 2005.

Levitt, Steven. *Freakonomics: A Rogue Economist Explores the Hidden Side of Everything.* New York: William Morrow, 2005

Luckham, David. *The Power of Events: An Introduction to Complex Event Processing in Distributed Enterprise Systems.* Boston, MA: Addison-Wesley Professional, 2002.

Mulholland, Andy; Thomas, Chris S.; Kurchina, Paul. *Mashup Corporations: The End of Business as Usual.* New York, NY: Evolved Technologist Press, 2007.

Pirsig, Robert. *Lila: An Inquiry into Morals.* New York: Bantam Books, 1991.

Pirsig, Robert. *Zen and the Art of Motorcycle Maintenance: An Inquiry into Values.* New York: Morrow, 1974.

Tapscott, Don. *Digital Capital: Harnessing the Power of Business Webs.* Boston, Mass.: Harvard Business School Press, 2000.

Wilson, Brian. *Systems: Concepts, Methodologies and Applications.* 1990. Chichester, UK: John Wiley & Sons, 1990.

Printed in the United Kingdom
by Lightning Source UK Ltd.
131849UK00002B/360/A